To My Grandchildren

So you might know a bit of your heritage.

Blessings

Tales of Trails in the Far North

An Alaskan Trapper's Journey

Mike Potts

Copyright © 2018 by Mike Potts

All rights reserved. This book or any portion thereof may not be reproduced or used in any form or by any electronic or mechanical means including information storage and retrieval systems without permission from the copyright holder, except by a reviewer, who may quote brief passages in a review.

Library of Congress Control Number: 2018940601

ISBN: 978-0-9977477-0-6

First Printing: May, 2018

Published by: 102nd Place, LLC
       Scottsdale, AZ

Table of Contents

Introduction 1
The Fall Hunt of '72 7
To Make A Toboggan 25
Journal of a Trapper 43
Last Season on the Trapline 81
   Appendix 115
Free Trappers I've Known 119
Vision of a Sodbuster 125

Introduction

Tales of Trails in the Far North is a compilation of the time when I was blessed to follow my vision of the "free" life in the land of the far north. These stories take place on the Yukon River long before much of the land was chopped up by various governmental and private Native Corporations. It's difficult now to wander around freely, set up a trapline, or build a few cabins without being served a trespass notice. As I look back on that time, I now realize that me, and others like me, were hungry for "FREEDOM;" freedom to fulfill our desire of life out and away from others.

In doing so I imagine some would consider us outlaws and selfish. We were about as free as anyone in my generation could have been but the life was never easy. When you're young though, you forget the tough times and "sally forth" as they used to say, hungry for more! I'm now 67 going on 68 (perhaps I will be 68 by the time this is published) and I've been asked many times, "Do ya miss that old free life?" My answer is yes. I stop and think on those days some; then I get up and do something.

One of those somethings was to sit down and write this book so those days would never be forgotten.

Journal of a Trapper was, of course, written while I was on the trapline in the early 70s. The other stories were written much later and spaced out. That's why you may read descriptions of things more than once but it also means you can start with any story in the book and still get the full feel of what things were like in the Alaska wilderness. Last Season on the Trapline was written in the winter of 1989/90 when I was laid up with a broken leg that I got in a logging accident. I wrote Vision of a Sodbuster in the winter of 2007/08 while taking care of my father in Arizona. The Fall Hunt of '72 and Free Trappers I've Known both where completed in the spring of 2009 as my family and I were on our island waiting for break up.

Since then my family has wandered many places in the world. We left Eagle, Alaska in 1989 traveling to Wyoming in our stock truck with our three workhorses because I saw that mini-series "*Lonesome Dove*" and thought I'd sure like to experience the west. So we headed there and lived in a wall tent a good part of the year in the mountains logging with my horses. I sold my sawmill which gave me enough to buy a house trailer in Encampment, Wyoming. This was the first home my wife had ever had with hot and cold running water and a washer and dryer. When the snow got deep we'd winter there. I still burned wood and I worked on ranches.

We enjoyed that life. The hunting was good too. I liked the country and the people; they were much like the Alaskans. But the Lord had some other plans for us.

I got ordained there and did some preaching. A little Ahtna Indian Church in Copper Center, Alaska heard about my ordination and asked us to come up. They wanted me to be the Pastor for their Church. So after five years and some internal struggles we loaded up the horses and headed north again

I bought another sawmill and logged and cut lumber to sell to supplement what they could pay us for pastoring. They were good people and we stayed there seven years from 1994 to 2000. The internet finally came to that part of Alaska in 1997. I spent some time with an old guy by the name of Max Fancher. He and his wife went to Mongolia each year for three summers to teach English. Communism had fallen in 1990 there in Mongoland and the country ran into "starvin' times." The Mongols are the toughest and most resourceful people I've come on.

Well I didn't know much about computers back then so I asked Max to send an email to a missionary there that he knew by the name of Rick Leatherwood. I'd seen a *National Geographic* with a photo article about those rugged herdsmen and I wanted to go there. So Max asked in the letter if Rick would help me find a couple Mongols. I was hoping one would know English and we'd go the Mongol way a-horse back to way out where they never heard of Christ. After a few months of persistent pushing my idea on him, he said ok come on over. The Church in Copper Center let me have a month off to go there.

Well he knew an ex-drunken horse thief that recently

turned to Christ and a streetwise kid that recently learned some English who could be a translator. We'd go out in a jeep (no real roads or bridges back then) travel 500 miles or so northeast where we'd buy horses then wander cross-country back to the capitol. It was over 500 miles stopping and staying with families in the herdsman tents. We'd tell them about God who came down from heaven and became a man, Jesus the Christ, to make man right with God. I admit adventure was probably first on my mind. Mongolia is much like the west was in the 1890s complete with horse thieves but I knew there were probably some there that God wanted. The only way to get them was to go and tell them about the One who paid their debt of sin and rose again.

Me and my two Mongol buddies did that for three years. Then in 2000 I moved there with my wife to a village four days a-horse back or a tough day by four-wheel drive. The village was Batshireet about 30 miles south of the Russian border. The country was much like central Montana: big grass-covered valleys and rolling, timbered mountains. God raised up a little group of Believers in that village so He started a work with us there. We took our sawmill and logging outfit and our horse farming tools and built a cabin. We became part of the community.

These were Buriot Mongols. Many of them looked like Navahos. Learning the language was a little tough but we did it. My ol' wife who was used to livin' in a one room log cabin cooking on a wood stove and packing water did just fine. In fact she misses those days in Mongoland. Life has changed there since then, like it does in all places. It's easier now that they have electricity and cell phones. Not as many are a-horse back these days. Seems wherever I go those good ol' days disappear so all I can do now is thank God for those days of freedom and talk about them.

In 2007 we had to come home and take care of my father till he died in August of 2008. We sold our place in Mongolia. Now here we are moving between an island in a big lake in northeast Minnesota near Canada, Alaska where our daughter lives with her three teenage kids, Arizona, and Mexico. I still get to preach some and disciple a few fellas. I've developed some bible studies to send to Mongolia. Every once in a while we go there as well as to India.

But we've grown old. I thank God I can still pack a canoe across a portage and paddle all day but my mountain man days are just a memory. I hope you enjoy these stories of me and my family's life in the Alaska wilderness. There'll always be those who seek freedom on the frontier. I hope they can find it somewhere and maybe find Christ too along the way.

The Fall Hunt of '72

On the banks of the Yukon River I sat on a bench in the Han village named Eagle Village. I was sewing "dog packs" out of canvas for my three malamute sled dogs. It was the first part of September and I was about to head out to the North Fork of the Fortymile River where my trapline was. September was the time to "make meat."

I was going to pack the dogs as well as myself, so was sewing under the instruction of an old lady of the village that grew up in the mountains along the Canada/Alaska border. When there wasn't snow they packed their dogs. She knew well how to make dog packs. So there I sat sewing and listening to some of the old-timers talk about their years wandering the bush in search of fur or meats as the Yukon rolled by.

There was a gravel mountain road that winded 161 miles north from the Alaska Highway to Eagle. It was open from mid-April till snows come in mid-October. I had that old lady's son drive me and the dogs out the road about seventeen miles to American Summit. It's at the timberline and I'd be walking west through the mountains about twenty-five miles to where the upper cabin was, then follow Comet Creek to north fork of the

Fortymile, turn right and follow it two miles up to the mouth of Eureka Creek and up a mile or so to my "Main cabin" on the trapline. That was about seventeen miles (42 miles altogether).

It was the first time I'd ever packed dogs and it was to be a learning experience. Keeping them balanced was of first importance and second, keeping them from wandering into bushes. They each had 35 or so pounds and I was packing a 70-pound pack. It's a rugged trail – lots of brush, soft ground, and steep ups and downs that were usually solid and rocky – thank God.

We started off early, drove up to American Summit and got the dogs and me packed. I grabbed my gun and with an "adios" I took off. About four months later I'd mush into Eagle before Christmas. The hills or mountains names were first, Mini Cup which we walked over then passed under Arkansas, then over Oregon on toward Glacier Mountain where Comet Creek starts and there's a trapline cabin there. Actually there are two routes to that cabin from Arkansas. You can go up a divide and then go down Bear Creek a ways then up a ridge – cross another side creek of Bear – top another divide that then drains into Comet Creek and work your way down to the cabin. That's really the best way but it takes a half-day longer. I'd usually camp on Bear Creek and get to the cabin the next day.

The other route is to follow a ridge with huge ups and downs till you go right over the top of Oregon then follow a ridge to the east fork of Comet, cross another ridge, then drop down to Comet and cross it to the cabin. That route is all above timber and very tough. The time we took the route over Oregon we left the road before eight in the morning. I don't believe we got there till after midnight; had a few problems with dogs and pack slipping or getting tangled in the brush. There was, as I remember, a moon out that cold September night so I could see pretty good. Even though I was young and tough, that was a haul. The dogs and I were pretty glad when we reached that cabin. We didn't get up too early the next morning. Twenty-five mountain miles are a whole lot different than twenty-five flat trail miles. As I remember we didn't do much the next day – just cleaned around the cabin and cut wood. Trapline cabins are usually ten to twelve miles apart.

This country opened up in the late 1800s to 1900. The cabin sites were used regularly till World War II. Then the country got plum lonely – no prospectors and the price of fur was down. However, there was one fella named Eric Staa that wintered here in the early 60s. He was a hand with an axe. He rebuilt what I called the upper, lower (on Comet Creek) and the Main cabin on Eureka Creek. I built one six miles below the upper cabin across the creek from a moose lick. I thought it would be a good place to "make meat."

The old-timers had a meat cache there and I made a new one. The moose lick is a spring that runs out to make a little creek that has a mineral salt in it but what they lick is the dirt. The moose got the banks all dug up and the spring is muddied up like a cow pen. Later years I shot a bunch of caribou and another year a fat bull moose. He was pawing at the banks and licking it up when I shot him. Anyway that year we'd get our meat off the North Fork . . . but I'm getting ahead of myself.

The next day we went as far as Moose Lick cabin. I needed to work on the roof some and do some other things. I might as well explain what a trapline cabin consists of. They are made of log, have a dirt floor, and a pole roof with dirt. They're about 9' x 9' and just high enough to stand up in. Inside there was a sheet metal stove about 30" x 16" x 12," a table in one corner, a bench, and across the back of the cabin was a pole bunk padded with grass with a piece of canvas or dried caribou hide on it. Each cabin I had outfitted with two cups, two plates, eatin tools, frying pan, spatula, two pots, and one big pot to melt snow for water or in the fall to pack water from the creek. I also had a sleeping bag in each cabin as well as an axe and a bow saw for firewood.

There was a good cache at upper and Main cabins. I kept flour, rice, etc. in them. The caches were built by cutting the tops out of two trees about 20 feet up. The trees needed to be about 14" in diameter. You make a ladder to top off the trees then make a platform out of poles between them. The platform is three feet below the "topped" trees. The triangle braces need to run above the platform so bears won't bust them and make the whole thing fall down. Then you build a miniature log cabin on the platform.

The best protection for bears not going into your

cabin and destroying things is taking everything out and putting it in your cache. Then leave the cabin door open so the bears feel welcome. They'll go in, look around, and punch out the window plastic then leave. If you shut the door, Mr. or Mrs. Bear will be right put out feeling unwelcome. They'll tear things up pretty good. I learned that the hard way.

The next day we went on down-stream to the mouth of Comet Creek. There's a big beaver pond there. We worked around it and went up the North Fork of Fortymile River. With hip boots I can cross at the riffles and walk from gravel bar to gavel bar. At the mouth of Eureka Creek we went up the creek about one-half mile to what I called the Main cabin. Home sweet home! This was the first place I could really call my mine. It was a little bigger than the others 10' x 12' and had a gable roof that extended three feet in front which made a nice little porch. Back in July when I'd been out there doing some trail work and such like, I dug out the floor about a foot then ripped out some logs with my chainsaw and put in a board floor. A dirt floor gets dried out and dusty real bad if you stay at a cabin for several days at a time.

I based my trappin operations out of here. A plane was coming in a week to "air drop" my grub and some dog food. I would pack this in my cache. Later with the dogs and a toboggan I would haul some to the line cabins to supply them and put in a good supply at the upper cabin.

Both Comet Creek and Eureka Creek run through

nice wide valleys. This part of the North Fork also runs through a nice wide valley all the way to the middle fork of Fortymile. All three you can cut out a trail that can keep you off the creeks most of the time. The hills and ridges between Eureka and Comet Creeks peek out above timberline. It starts at the heads of those creeks in the Glacier Mountains which are big old rugged glacier-carved mountains with Dall sheep runnin around them. There's of course lots of gnarly Black Spruce timber, but there's good patches of hillside Birch, patches of Aspen, Willow, and along the creeks there are many patches of good straight White Spruce too. Of course there's "the Bush," the Alaska wilderness sometimes called tangle foot because it's so tough to get through. The buck bush in particular causes problems.

Well I set up the wood stove in the cabin and got a fire going to make some tea and something to eat. I still had some dried salmon for the dogs. That's sure a pretty and peaceful place; you can hear Eureka Creek runnin across the riffles. It's not real closed-in with timber so you can see the hills around pretty good. And I've always thought Eureka Creek water was the best tasting water around. After packing things from the cache to move back into the cabin the day was pretty well used up. I had chain spots with dog houses. There were two five-gallon cans of kerosene for the couple railroad lanterns I used for light at the Main cabin. I burned candles at the other line cabins. We were setup pretty good and the cabin was warm. I had three or four days till the plane came with the air drop so I cut a lot of wood in sled-length and stacked it so we could haul the firewood with the dogs after the snow comes.

I used the Warbelow's Air Ventures out of Tok, Alaska for my airdrops. They flew with the door off of their Cesena 206. There was a big "Tussock Flat" out back of the cabin that made a good drop target. For those of you who might not know, a tussock flat is a piece of permafrost ground that only moss grows on. The moss heaves up and walkin on it is like trying to walk through a plowed field. But it's easy to spot from the air. They flew low and slow with flaps on and someone in back to pitch out two or three packs at a time. These "packs" were packed rock-hard and tied up with strapping tape. If they were a little loose they'd blow out on impact. When the pilot yelled "*pitch um*" the guy in the back would. They'd circle around and do it again till all was out. Then they'd wave their wings at me. They were the last people I'd see till I'd go back to Eagle just before Christmas.

I'd be counting the packs they'd drop and then have to go find them all. Some would actually slide under the moss and be out of sight. Fortunately the streamers would help locate them. After gathering all the packs I'd start hauling them to the cache or cabin. Warbelow's would drop early in morning and I'd be packing all day.

With that finally done I could start hunting for winter's meat. It must have been around September 13th. There was frost in morning and I knew in about three weeks "freeze up" would start in earnest. I decided to pack the dogs and myself and go up to the Moose Lick cabin to hunt around there. We left early in the morning and started down Eureka Creek to North Fork. I noticed a lot of fresh moose tracks along the river. I got down to the beaver pond at the mouth of Comet Creek and on the other side was a "barren" cow moose (means she didn't have a calf). I dropped my pack, threw my 30/06 up to my shoulder and squeezed off a shot. She wasn't more than 120 yards. I hit her in the back part of her lungs but she didn't drop. She went into the pond! Just about then Ranger, my lead dog, jumped in after her with his pack on. I didn't want to shoot her there but she started after Ranger so I shot her in the head.

That water was cold; there was ice on the edge. All I had was a two-foot piece of rope. I cut down a pole-size spruce and tied one end of the rope to the pole. When I got out to her, I punched a hole in her ear, and tied the other end of the rope there. The pond was chest deep. I drug her till she bottomed out, then I gutted her where she lay. It's no fun in cold water. She was fat being she had no calf and a fat moose was just what we needed. I chopped her in half just behind the ribs, that way I could pull one-half up almost out of the water. I skinned the first half, quartered it and got the meat on dry land. Then I did the same to the other half. Really I didn't actually quarter it. I did cut the legs off, ribs, rump, and so on. I ended up with ten pieces.

After that I had to go back to the Main cabin to get spikes, nails, wire and rope to make a cache right there at the beaver pond. I was cold and hungry. By then it must've been 10:30 a.m. or so. I took the dogs back with some meat and guts for us to eat. I chained Oddball and Patches up and decided to take Ranger back with me in case of bears. I got some dry clothes on but the inside of my hip boots were still wet. Ate something then headed back to make the cache. I'd already found two big spruce growing close together.

The first thing I did was chop down two dry spruce poles about 4" on the butt and cut them about 16' long. I cut another pole in 2' lengths then split them with an axe for the ladder rungs. I put a notch in the sixteen foot poles every sixteen inches or so to nail the rungs in. Next I braced the ladder on first one, and then the other, of the close together spruce to chop off their branches so the trees were clean all the way up the height of the ladder. Then I found a good stout pole the right size to go between the trees as a cross-pole and hold the weight of the meat. I cut it and packed it back to the cache, tied a long rope to it, then climbed up the ladder and pulled it up with heavy telegraph wire. (A telegraph line had run from Valdez, Alaska. to Fort Egbert next to Eagle City during the gold rush days so it was easy to find wire where the poles had fallen down.) I rapped it about three times and twisted her tight to the tree. Then I put the ladder on the second tree and tied the rope to the other end of the cross-pole, pulled her up, and wired it to the tree just like the opposite side.

With that preparation done I put the ladder against the cross-pole. I would tie the rope to one of the pieces of meat, as well as a short piece of thinner rope, so when I pulled the meat up I could tie it to pole. But I'm getting ahead of myself. By the time I got the cache done it was nigh onto dark. I'd leave the meat on the ground one night and hang it up first thing in the morning. I was young and this was only my second year on the trapline. I was still learning and making mistakes along the way.

Anyway, me and Ranger headed home. At a bend on the North Fork before Eureka Creek we saw a huge bull moose in the twilight. Ranger took off after it. Well they ran up the gravel bar and on out into the river. The moose stood there in about three feet of water in the middle of the rapids. Ranger was on the edge of the river barking at the moose. I crossed over to the side the moose was on then walked the gravel bar up to where they were in a "stand-off." (The water is a moose's protection against wolves.) Well the bull saw me and crossed over to the other side, which is the side Eureka Creek is on. So I thought, *I want two moose for me and the dogs, so what am I waiting for?* I threw up my rifle and looked through my scope. I could see the crosshairs of the scope on the bull's rib cage so I pulled the trigger. I could see I hit it good. It wandered off into the bush. Unfortunately ol Ranger took off after it and turned it back around. It came back to the river and started across toward me but when it got right in the middle of the rapids it fell over dead! Again I was faced with a moose in the water. It was deep, over my hip boots. Still I went out and grabbed the horns. I leaned back and the moose floated a little toward shore. I stepped back again and it floated in some more I did this several times till the moose grounded out. Then I spread-eagled him, slit his belly, and stared pulling guts.

It was dark now. I had two moose down and being that I was alone I had a heap of work ahead of me. I made sure that the bull couldn't float away then me and Ranger headed for home. I was tired, wet, and hungry. Ranger's head was a whole lot higher than mine. I forgot to say when the bull went down Ranger swam out to it, climbed on, and started biting. Hair was flying! I guess that's a dog's way of counting coup.

Looking back, now that I'm next door to 60 years of age, I know I couldn't do that again. I have a little more wisdom in such matters. Then I was young and everything was fairly new and exciting. I was learning a trade I had dreamed about growing up in Iowa. I had a lot of preconceived ideas that experience would eventually correct. It'd take another year before I would begin to be getting good at it.

So now we had two moose down. The closest was a mile below Main cabin; the other I still had to hang. The next morning I put on my wet hip boots and headed down to the beaver pond. I decided a couple or three hours more wouldn't hurt that bull in the 33 degree water. It wasn't going anywhere I went on down and started packing the cow moose to the cache a piece at a time. Like I said I'd tie a lighter rope to each piece to secure the meat to the cross-pole. The long rope I would tie to each piece, climb up the ladder with the rope in my hand, pull the meat up, tie it on cross-pole, then untie the long rope and do it all again till all ten pieces were tied to the cross-pole. I did something wrong as you'll see later.

With that job done I went back and started skinning and cutting up the bull. It was real fat. It was gonna be like eating prime beef. I skinned it and cut the legs, ribs, rump, neck, and backbone off and laid each piece on the brush so I wouldn't get sand and gravel on the meat. Counting the head there were ten pieces to pack to the Main cabin. Round trip of two miles times ten pieces meant 20 miles to pack that moose. The hind legs were the heaviest, maybe 120 lbs.

I took the rump home that night. It had three inches of fat on it; didn't want a bear to enjoy it. It was a gamble if a grizzly would get the rest but you can only do so much. I fried some tenderloin steaks up in moose fat and made some biscuits and gravy and a quart of tea. When ya work hard fancy grub don't get it; just lots gets it. It takes a lot of calories to keep ya goin when you work like that. I slept good and in the morning after a stack of hotcakes and steaks I was ready to start packin the bull in.

I always took Ranger with me and had my rifle wherever I went. I got to where the bull was to find it gone! Just kidding, it was all there and okay except for Camp Robber (Canada Jays) and Raven poop on some of it. It was a mile to cabin so I found some down trees and such to rest on. I'd probably rest two to three times a trip. Ten trips with heavy packs plus hanging them in the cache I had made in the summer wears you out after time. Crossing the North Fork too I'd have to be careful not go over my hip boots. I'd cross on the riffles which run diagonally across the river. I think I still had two or three pieces the following day; it takes time packing and hanging them since the pieces probably weighed 120 pounds or more. I was a little tired and didn't do much for a couple days.

One of those mornings I was woke up by the dogs woofing, I stepped outside to see them looking on the downstream side of the cabin. About 100 feet away was a cow moose! I heard something on the upstream side too. It was a bull about to cross the creek. My first thought was to grab my rifle, but then realized I didn't need any more meat so I just enjoyed watching them instead. They slowly crossed the creek, climbed the bank on other side, crossed the flat, then up the hill, and disappeared.

The work was done – the pressure of getting meat for winter was over. Praise God! Back then, I didn't know or care about God or fear Him. Fact is, it all belongs to God and He controls all things according to His will whether we like it or not. We can be so foolish to think God is wrong and get angry or be dumb enough not to realize we are in His hand. Proverb 16:9 says, *"In the heart man plans his way, but God directs his steps."* Later God would have mercy on the wretched man that I am and saw I wasn't ready to step into eternity a sinner and without knowing that Jesus is my Lord and savior. That was going to be some years later.

Now I'd best go see how the meat was at the beaver pond. This time I took Oddball. I named him that when he was about six months' old cuz he was the oddest looking pup I'd seen. He was white as a cue ball hence Oddball, but now he was getting as big as Ranger and Patches. With his winter coat of fur he was a mighty fine-looking dog. Later as Ranger got too old to work Oddball became my lead dog and companion.

He got to have a certain amount of notability in the Eagle area. He could "break out" a sled packed with seven or eight 100lbs sacks of dog food, line a canoe up a river, tackle a wounded Caribou and hold it till you got there to finish it off, and was as friendly a dog as you'd find. Oh and a few years later when I was "ratting" up the Porcupine River, on some lakes the ice was off the edges but I couldn't use the canoe yet, I'd shoot Muskrats with a .22 and he'd retrieve them. At about 12-years-old he succumbed to cancer. It was winter. By then I'd quit the trapline and was homesteading with horses so had quit a pile of manure. The ground was froze so I shot him to put him out of his misery and buried him in the manure. He later fed us with the potatoes that we grew on the land we spread him on. He was quite a dog.

Well we got down to the beaver pond and I could see that something wasn't right. Not all the meat was hanging on the pole. I hoped that maybe the cord broke and it fell on the ground but no that wasn't it. I found grizzly sign all over the place and the bark on the trees was torn up. There were only four pieces of meat left. I was tired of packing yet that's what I'd have to do. I mistakenly thought back then that grizzlies couldn't climb trees and the meat was too close to trees.

That night I stayed on the other side of the beaver pond where I could see the meat; the grizzly never came. I got what was left. Over the years I tried to cache moose and caribou but I lost several to bears. There was one cache in particular. Me and Bill Goebel had shot six caribou and had made a cache we hoped was "bear proof." The trees were wide enough apart and the cross-pole was six inches at the small end. Even on a ladder you couldn't reach out and touch the closest pieces from either end. There was almost two feet to spare. You couldn't stand under it either holding your rifle by the butt and touch it. Well we left it there thinking it'll be there when we mush out with the dogs after freeze up. We didn't get back till first part of December. What we found was one end of the cross-pole on the ground and not one piece of meat left! A grizzly had shinnied up one tree and chewed the cross-pole like a beaver! It must have camped there till all the meat was gone.

Fortunately that year caribou were wintering along the North Fork and on up Slate Creek (where we cached the caribou). We shot a couple for fresh meat. It was a good thing cause we didn't have any thanks to Mr. Griz. They aren't punching a time-clock; it's obvious that bear couldn't get at that meat. I'm sure it took him a while to figure a way to get it. Was it luck or thinking on his part to climb up the tree that the small end of cross-pole was spiked on and chew through it?

I was married by this time to one of the girls from Eagle Village, a Han Indian. Her father trapped that country in the 1930s. We'd just had our first daughter so that year I made trips alone with my dog team out to run trapline every week or so. It was cold in '77, often the temperature was 60 below.

Anyway back to 1972, that fall it was freezing every night from about the 20th of September on. Even though Mr. Griz got most of the cow moose I still thought we'd be okay. I got things ready for I still had four weeks or so till I'd set out traps. I had plans to hunt at the moose lick but as you can see I didn't need to. On another frosty morning, can't remember when for sure but probably the first week in October, I saw something black moving around but not going anywhere. I watched it a while and saw it was a black bear grazing on frozen blueberries. After they freeze they're real sweet. Blueberry fattened black bear is good groceries.

So I put on my hip boots and crossed the creek. The wind was blowing lightly toward me and by moving slightly south of east I was out of sight of the bear. Once I'd get to the hill on the other side of the creek I'd side hill around and be in range. The bear was across the creek northeast from the cabin, up a small valley. For an interior Alaskan Black Bear this was good size – about 170 pounds. One shot took care of it. The meat was fat, the guts were fat; I'd make some good lard. As I think back I tied a rope around its neck then had

Patches and Ranger pull the bear to the cabin. The ground was mossy with frost too so it pulled easy. I had an easy time skinning and cutting up the bear. Now I could have a little variety in my life. Instead of moose, biscuits, and gravy, I could have bear, biscuits, and gravy. Sometimes I'd boil up some pinto beans and bake some bread.

The meat was made, I just now needed to cut wood and wait for freeze up so I could start trapping. Ya know you work hard it's amazing how much meat you'll eat. I did mix some up with the dog feed and cooked it for the dogs. (The next year I had me a canoe and a couple gillnets and would catch dog salmon and whitefish for dog feed and have it air-dropped in the fall.) As I said I was still learning and everything was still new and exciting to me.

Now I'm about 60-years-old and got those memories to think on. We did the trapline life through all of the 1970s. I'm sure there are other young men full of dreams of adventures in the north. I hope they'll get to see their dreams come to reality. The north was still wild and free back then. I don't think it's so free now. But just the same, good huntin to ya and may you recognize God's hand in your life.

To Make A Toboggan

In my early years of becoming a Mountain Man, the first teacher I had for running a trapline and running dog teams used sleds. He was in the Talkeetna Mountains and ran the creeks and rivers there. They would run a lot "overflow" on top of the ice. That's when the springs that feed them build up pressure, crack the ice and run water on top of the ice till the pressure settles down. Then that water freezes up till the pressure builds again, cracking the ice and repeating the process. This happens throughout the winter. From time to time you'll be running a sled through water on top of good ice. Usually just a few inches but sometimes it might be knee high. Sleds are better for that because you only have two, two-inch runners to knock and scape ice off of.

"Poly-plastic" for both sleds and toboggans came out in the late '70s and this revolutionized mushing. You could generally run into water then back onto snow and keep going without the snow freezing on the bottom; which of course used to drag and slow you down as well as wear your dogs out. When I moved to the eastern Alaskan interior, Eagle Village on the Yukon River, I learned from old-time trappers the toboggan with a single file line of dogs pulling was preferred over sleds. Even though overflow on creeks and then going onto snow was a problem before poly-plastic, it was still better for trapping for several reasons. First it made a flat smooth trail that was solid enough to walk on, whereas a sled trail wasn't solid and always was tough to walk on. Second, you could break out a trail with snowshoes that the dogs and toboggan could follow. And third, it tracked better with a load than a sled. You'd have to use a "gee pole" with a sled to keep it on a trail.

After ice was out on the Yukon, I asked an old guy in the Indian village of Eagle where I stayed in the summers, to go with me to a stand of birch I had heard about below Eagle Bluff. The reason was to find straight-grained birch to split with an axe and then later I'd hew it out and plane the pieces into boards to make a toboggan for next winter. His name was Jacob Malcolm. This was the summer of '73 so Jake must have been in his mid-50s. He grew up in the "bush" as a kid and lived most of his young life in a wall tent. Some years he and his family didn't even come to the river, they just lived off the land. Only the father came to sell fur for the few supplies they needed. They always used toboggans.

I had a canoe that summer; used it mainly to check a gillnet that I used to feed me and my dog team during the summer. Then in the first half of September, I would catch dog salmon for winter dog feed. One evening, Jake and I shoved off in the canoe to find a couple straight-grain birch trees. Now birch is the closest thing to hardwood in the "Far North" so that's what we use. It's daylight 24/7 in June and July so it's nice working at night. Mosquitoes ease up a bit and it's cooler. So off we went with a coffee can with a wire bail handle, two cups, tea and sugar, and an axe.

After leaving the village we floated/paddled about three miles to Eagle City; that's where the white folks live. Back then, there were thirty-five or so living there but Eagle Village had the school with grades 1 through 8. The white kids would have to go up there to school and the folks would take turns driving them up the three mile dirt road. Eagle City had one General store and one "Roadhouse." It also had a post office. All the mail came by plane from Fairbanks once a week and then later it started coming three times a week. It's a pretty little burg with a lot of Klondike Gold Rush history. It rests next to Mission Creek, where the creek spills out into the Yukon. Eagle Bluff is on downriver side of the creek. The Bluff is high, craggy red rock with many draws going up it with aspen and some white spruce. Out in front, in the middle of the river is Bell Island. Standing on the bank in front of Eagle Bluff, there's a beautiful panoramic view of both downriver and upriver, as well as hills running into Canada just a few miles east.

Below Eagle Bluff a little ways back from the river, is a bench of land that has some birch of fair size. The river runs about six knots. We floated most of the way to where the birch stand was. It took less than an hour

27 To Make a Toboggan

to get there, but it would be longer going back up river. We landed the canoe, pulled it up on beach, and tied it to some willows. Then with axe in hand we went to the birch stand to find a straight-grain tree. You first got to find a straight one and it takes a lot of looking. From a distance many look good only to get right next to them looking on all three sides to find they are crooked or bowed. Once you've found one you take your sharp axe, and I mean sharp, and blaze off a piece of bark about a foot long. In the wood at the bottom of the blaze dig out the start of a shaving with your axe. Then with your hand pull up and see if it pulls straight. If it does it might be straight-grained. Chop it down close to the ground. As I said sharp axe and I meant it! The old-timers usually carried a round stone that they, from time to time, would take a blow from wood cutting and work the edge of the axe with the stone keeping it as sharp as any skinning knife. Any more there aren't axe men, what with chainsaws and such available, but back then the old-timers were still alive and willing to show someone interested in learning the trade.

If you start with a new axe it'll be petty blunt. If you sight down its edge you'll see what I call cheeks. Those need to be filed off, as well as the edge needs to be worked on with the file. Why they sell them that way I don't know, but you need a flatter angle with a sharp edge to do any work. It takes a lot of filing to get the axe ready for work. Start with a new file that will grab the steal and tear it off. If it just slides without grabbing you're wasting your time. Now let's get to work.

When a tree was down we'd measure it with the length of the axe – a trail axe is two feet. I was going to need a toboggan with a six foot bed. I'd need to add two feet more for the curl in front where the handle bars are and two feet behind the bed where you stand. The total then is ten feet. Actually, you need two logs cause you'll need three boards to make a toboggan. We chopped down several and tried to split them only to see them split crooked. We split them by starting at the butt of the log with the axe. When the log started to crack length-wise we'd put one of the wedges in that we made from a pole-sized dead spruce. Pounding it a few times with a pole about two feet long till it was in the crack deep enough to take the axe out. Then we'd continue driving it in and watch how it split. If it's splitting straight, we'd continue with a second wedge. We'd keep on using one wedge then the next till it splits in two.

Now I said it took several logs till we got two logs to split straight. Probably was about 1:00 or 2:00 a.m. The sun had made a full circle. It never does get dark and the sun only dips down below the northern horizon out of sight for a couple hours in June. Finally we had the four pieces we needed. We then "rough-hewed" them down flat on the outside. It makes them lighter. We do this by finding a couple trees growing close together and wedge one of the pieces at a time between the trees about two feet off the ground. Then with the axe we'd mark the round side by striking once every two inches. The strikes sink in about an inch or so. Then starting at

29 To Make a Toboggan

one end we'd chop out what we'd "striked" and continue until it gets down to about two inches thick. The strikes guide you so you're more consistent in the depth you hew off. We did that to all four pieces. I'd finish them up back at the village. By the time we finished the striking and packed them to the river it was probably 3:00 a.m.

We kicked up a fire and put on a pot of old, silty river water for tea. We sat around, drank tea, and ate some Pilot crackers and dry fish. It was close to 4:00 a.m. by the time we shoved off. We can't paddle against the six knot current so we lined up. This can be done one of three ways. First, if alone you need a 40 foot rope. One end is tied to the bow and the other to the stern with you on the beach holding the point of the triangle. You adjust where you should hold the rope so the bow is a little farther out from the beach than the stern. That way the current keeps the canoe away from shore. It moves up river as you are walking and pulls fairly easy. A keel helps it track better.

The second way is with two guys – one steering in the stern and the other on shore. You tie one end to the middle thwart and tie in the other end a big bowline knot. The guy pulling from the beach puts the knot over his head and under the arm that's nearest the canoe. Then he starts walking. The canoe will want to go out away from shore. The guy steering will have the paddle on the shore side of the canoe steering it straight with the bow pointed up river. Again it does not pull too hard. If you have a load you'll need to tie the rope to the thwart just behind the front seat or the weight will make it hard to steer. The current has too much leverage if you don't move the rope more toward the bow.

The third way is with one or two dogs. The best harness is a cut seams burlap sack. Cut it at the seams and lay it out then start at one corner and roll it up kitty-corner so the roll will be long enough (needs to be 100 pound size sack). The rolled up sack goes over the dog's neck on the side away from canoe and between the front legs then over the back. You tie the two ends of the sack together and then attach it to the rope tied to canoe. You'll be using your lead dog so get in canoe and tell the dog to "*get.*" He'll start out upriver at a good trot. If he comes to a driftwood pile you say "*come here.*" He'll come out in the water a little away from the driftwood pile and then you say "*get*" and he starts pulling upriver again. When you run out of beach on one side you load your dog in or make him swim and you paddle to the other side. Now you've a current so you'll drift some and lose some ground. Can't be helped just get going to other side and line up till you run out of beach and have to cross again.

Well this time I was the dog and Jake steered. After we shoved off we paddled to the other side since the beach was better for lining. There was only one slough to cross and then we were on the riverside of Pete Londean's Island. The island was at low water connected to land so we at that time couldn't go up the slough but at the downriver end it had enough water that I got in and we paddled across. Then we had clear good beach for about a mile then a big bluff, so we had to cross the river again and line up that side to the village. Like I said you lose some ground paddling across, maybe a quarter mile. Lining is slow so if time means something to ya you'd best throw your watch away so you won't have time to worry about.

   Then we had only two miles left to the village. I imagine it was 6:00 or 6:30 in the morning. Most everyone was still sleeping in the village, except for a couple old-timers sitting on a bench watching the morning come on the river. I can't remember for sure, but probably after unloading the wood and beaching the canoe we cooked up some pancakes. I ate a lot of them in those days. We went to bed and slept some. Jake, he was a good sleeper, probably slept like a bear. As I said he grew up in a wall tent and remembered the life in bush Alaska before World War II. Things were the same as it was in 1898 (more or less). Steamboats were the connection to the outside world till 1950 or so in the Eagle part of the Yukon. The mail plane didn't take over the dog team mail route till close to World War II. Jake loved life on the trapline but hadn't been doing that since back then. Oh he played around at it near the village and did some hunting and fishing.

   He finally took another young fella from the village a couple years after I made this toboggan. By then I'd made another one so he fixed my old one, got some traps and an outfit, and the two of them trapped a couple seasons on Champion Creek southwest of Eagle. Later on he somehow caught T.B. I'd been married several years to a gal from the village and had a couple kids. We'd quit the trapline and started a Sawmill by then. I'd heard Jake was sick, then later heard he looked like a walking skeleton. I went to see him and found out he had T.B. but he was spooked of doctors and wouldn't go to Fairbanks. That was till I told him if he didn't he was going to die. That spooked him more so he went on the mail plane to the Fairbanks hospital. He was too weak to walk by that time. It ended that it was too late and he died in the hospital. I think he was in his 60s – sad. He was the last of the "Old-Timers" that lived the old-time bush livin along the Upper Yukon. He and other old-timers showed me some of the old skills that I'm passin on to you all.

Well it was time to make good boards out of those slabs. I bought a good jack plane and had a good sharp trail axe, so went to work. First I had to keep hewing them down with the axe till they were about an inch thick, then edge them with the axe, then plane them smooth and square. They looked like boards now. The front three feet had to be planed down to a ½ an inch because that had to be bent up for the front. I had now two 5" boards and one 4" board. A fourteen inch wide toboggan is the right width for fall time shallow snow cause the wider the toboggan the more you'll get stuck in tight places. A sixteen inch width is nice but you need real good trails then.

You need some crosspieces to bolt through the long boards. Now in years gone by they used "babiche" (caribou rawhide) and laced it. What you'd do is at about a 45 degree angle drill a hole one-quarter inch then another hole at the same angle that will come through at the same exit hole on the underside of the toboggan boards. Then with soaked up babiche you lace it up. On the bottom the lacing is up inside the hole so it can't be torn or snagged on anything. When it's dry it's tight. Two lacings per board is good so across the crosspiece you'd have six lacings. That's the old way. I used bolts and drilled six holes per crosspiece and countersunk the bottom side with a pocket knife. I think I used $3/16^{th}$ flathead bolts with good washers and nuts on top of the crosspieces. You don't want the heads of the bolts flush with the bottom of the toboggan cause they wear down and then your bolt heads will be dragging. You'll need a crosspiece at both ends and one in front of your feet where you'll put the upright boards for the handlebars. You'll also need three more evenly spaced in between. The front of the toboggan needs to be angled down to about eleven inches across. That'll help you through tight spots or to get around a tree.

Once you have the boards bolted together you're ready to build a fire in your dog food cooker. I cut a 55 gallon drum on the ring down from the end that has the bung holes in. Then I set the end on the ground and about two inches down from the ring you cut out a twelve inch square. That's the door to put wood in. The ring you cut, take a sledge hammer and tap it in a bit. That's so you can put the other end of the drum on it with water in it and that's your dog food cooker.

However in this case, instead of dog food, you'll put

10 or 15 gallons of water on. Get the fire going underneath. When the water gets to boiling, put the front end of the toboggan in. You'll probably need to lean the other end on the fish cache so it won't tip over. You do have a fish cache don't you? Every ten minutes or so take it out put it in the bender (I don't know what else to call it).

You make the bender by taking a round, un-split piece of firewood about ten inches in diameter and on each end of it nail a 2x4. One end of each 2x4 should stick out from the firewood log about a foot. The other end sticks out about three feet. On the foot ends nail a 2x4 across them. That's the type of bender I used. It's simple and works. Put the front end of the toboggan in between the log and the cross 2x4 then start pushing down a little on the long ends. The first couple times just flex it a little then put it back into the hot water for a while. One of those times you should be able to push the levers past the toboggan bottom. Keep bending it till it's bent about a foot to fourteen inches up. In other words, if it was flat on the ground the nose of the toboggan would be fourteen inches high above ground. To keep the bend in, keep the toboggan in the bender till September. Just slide a pole between the levers and the toboggan bottom then tie them up so it won't slip.

In September take off the bender, drill two holes in the nose crosspiece in the center of the outside boards. I used telegraph wire which is about as thick as one of those fuzzy pipe cleaners maybe a 1/8" diameter. Run the wire in both holes from outside, cross them over and run them under next crosspiece on either side of the middle board then twist them together behind the crosspiece so they hold. Next take a six inch nail or something like that and where the wire crosses itself put in the nail and twist it tight. Then tie off the nail with thinner wire so it won't untwist. My father-in-law, he's an old trapper from that village, said to put the wire in the fire awhile first to take some of the temper out cause you from time to time bump into things and so it flexes often and will eventually break. Well I didn't and it did break but quite a while later.

Next we need to put handlebars on, so first you got to put the uprights in back; just in front of the crosspiece that's ahead of where you stand. The uprights are made with any 1x6 boards you have laying around, can be spruce or whatever, but if you don't you'll have to find a dead spruce with a straight crack running up it. You'll split it out and go through the same process as making toboggan boards from a birch. You are going to cut the boards about the length that would be comfortable for you to be holding onto handlebars. Now they're going to be wider at the top than on the bottom by about four inches. So say the toboggan bed is fourteen inches wide, your upper end will be eighteen inches wide. You'll have an upper and a lower cross-board to bolt the two uprights together. They should be 1x6 boards too. Just bolt them together. The crosspiece on the bed of the toboggan that you put the uprights next to needs to be thicker than others, a good two inches, because you'll need to drill four holes through where the uprights are bolted to it.

Now for the handlebars you need to do a little pole hunting in the woods to find ones that started out in life bent for the first few years. They should look like a lazy "j," the bent part should be about a foot long. Hew one side flat so it's rounded on the outside. These need to be long enough to run to the crosspiece that's up the toboggan from the one that the uprights are bolted to. It should be a little ways back of middle – reason being as toboggans continue to pack the snow down from snow fall to snow fall the trails get a little wavy. You don't want the handlebar attached to the bed of the toboggan too far forward or the bed will not float or snake over the waves in the trail. It will be too stiff. Now the bent end is sticking out past the uprights, being they're bent so they run flat out the back instead sticking up above the uprights at a 45 degree angle. Do you understand?

Lace the handlebar to the bed of the toboggan just back of the crosspiece. You put it there cause you will need to push the toboggan handlebars from time to time and you'll need to push against the crosspiece or you'll eventually break the lacing. You first drill two holes on the bottom of the toboggan that will exit at the same hole the pole is in about two inches in diameter. Cut at the angle so it will be flat to the bed, butted up to that crosspiece. Start the holes on each side of the handlebar angled so again they'll exit the same place on the bottom and then drill a horizontal hole through the handlebar above the other holes on the toboggan bed. Lace it tight with wet babiche.

Now you got the toboggan just about finished, but you need to drill a hole up in the nose of the toboggan so you can run three-quarter inch nylon rope though. That's what you're going to hook the dogs to. The hole should be one inch. The rope wraps around the uprights at the base and spliced into itself; it pulls good that way. You'll splice a ring in where you hook in the mainline that the dogs pull from. Now you need to kill a moose, cause you need the skin for the sides. If it's fresh killed that's ok; cut the hide in half length-wise. Next with a sharp knife cut about an inch of hair away from the edge of the hide. You're going need a bunch of one-half inch screws. Or if you have some one-quarter inch plywood you'd do better with one inch screws. The plywood you'll cut in one inch strips then start at the nose of the toboggan and screw the edge of the hide to the toboggan (the edge you cut the hair off). When you get to the back stop for a bit cause you need to drill a hole on the uprights next to the handlebars and one about an inch in from the upper edge of the nose. Take 3/8" rope, tie a knot in it at the end, then run the other end from the outside in through the hole in the nose then through the hole next to handlebars. Pull tight, then go around the handlebar and tie it tight to itself. Now you drape the hide folded over the rope, punch your knife through both under the rope, and lace it with babiche or rope, pulling it tight as you go. Both ends of the lace need to be attached to the nose and the uprights. Now screw the back edge of the hide to the uprights pulling it tight. With both sides done, you've one last important thing to make - a brake.

You might get going too fast down a hill and run your wheel dog over. What's a wheel dog? Oh, it's the dog just in front of the toboggan. Or the team may smell a moose and start running in the brush. There's many a time you'd bust your toboggan up if you don't have a good brake. Go buy an eight inch strap hinge and you need a #3 horseshoe. If ya can't weld, take it to a welder. Heat the heels of the shoe red-hot and bend them 90 degrees. They should stick down one and one-half inches. Grind them across so they got an edge that will dig in when you stand on it. Now weld the shoe on one side of the hinge, bent heels down of course. You'll need to weld a strap across the inside the shoe midway between heel and toe to the hinge.

Now that the brake is made you'll bolt the other part of the hinge to the middle board back where you stand, again on the bottom of the toboggan. With a pocket knife dig out the hole so the bolt head is well up in the wood. Bolt that side of the hinge down with the joint right even with the back end of the toboggan. That way with your toe you can flip it up between your feet when you don't need to brake. The toboggan is finished. Ain't it pretty!

You got maybe three to four weeks till you'll be loading up and ready to travel. That's good cause the hide needs to dry and lighten up. You can use a bull caribou hide, or Polly Duck canvas, but moose hide is tough.

Fall of '73, about the 16th of October it was staying

colder than 25 degrees and there was about six inches of snow. So I hitched up my "boys" with Ranger in the lead, Patches in swing, and Oddball in wheel. I had the old-fashioned dog harnesses on them. They were like horse harnesses; each had a collar, back-pad, and a bellyband with tugs on each side. The swing and wheel harnesses on the tugs had rings riveted in just above the back-pad. The tugs had snaps on the ends that would snap into the rings. The lead dog tugs snap into the tugs of the wheel and swing dogs, the swing dog's tugs snap into the wheel dogs tugs, then the wheel dog's tugs would snap into the single tree that was snapped into the toboggan tug.

Remember the rope you put through the hole in the nose of the toboggan you drilled? I had to have (and you will too) a rope that was tied to that ring. It's about fourteen feet. At about ten feet, tie a big ring in it, that way you take the tail end of the rope around a tree then tie a "jerk" knot to it. Why? You'll find out the first time you hitch those dogs that have been on dog chains most of the summer. They're eager to run and you won't get to the back of the toboggan before they take off. My dogs I train to lie down till I tell them to *"get"* but when they haven't run all summer I'll have a better start with that rope tied. There were some wood trails behind the village so we ran back there a mile or so. The toboggan held together, the dogs ran good, and Ranger geed and hawed good so I figured everything was a go for heading out to the trapline in a week or so. By the way you want your heavier stuff in the back of the toboggan. You'll learn as you go, use common sense, and you'll do fine. Happy trails.

Journal of a Trapper

September 17, 1973
Hazy but clear towards night

Got up about six this morning, had hotcakes and bacon. Then Oliver Lyman drove us up to the summit to start our walk to the upper end of my trapline to get our winter supply of meat. Dave Young, a greenhorn, came along. He is going to stay the winter in the upper cabin and learn the ways of northern mountains.

From about six miles out, ran into herds of caribou on all sides of us, some within twenty yards.

About ten miles out, ran into two biologists studying the caribou. Talked awhile and went on, still seeing caribou. I want to go over Mt. Oregon and make to cabin but not enough light, so dropped down Bear Creek and made camp. Ate a good supper of macaroni and cheese and Spam. Drank lots of tea. Went to sleep. (Distance traveled about 15 miles.)

September 18, 1973
Clear, freezing at night, rising to 50° or so in the day

Got up and got a fire going. Had rice cereal and tea.

Packed up, headed out. Went down Bear Creek to ridge running toward Comet Creek, where we're going.

Just before we got to the last ridge before Comet, we saw what thought was the last of the caribou. Dave shot a fairly fat cow, boned it out and went on. Only now with 70 or 80 lb. packs. Got over the hump looking down in Comet to see lots more caribou. We walked within a mile of the cabin and dropped our packs. Stalked two miles after two extremely large and fat bull caribou. After stalking them, laid down, watched them for a half hour and then moved in. Dave shooting one and me the other. After gutting them, went down, picked up the packs and went on to cabin. Boiled up caribou tongue and dried spuds and fried up kidneys and made gravy. Ate so much I couldn't stay awake, went to sleep.

September 19, 1973
Clear freezing at night, 40° or 50° in day

Well, this morning had bannock and fat rump steaks, hung all the cow in the meat cache. Then went up to where we shot the bulls, skinned them out, cut them up. Once in a while looking in case of grizzlies; only to see caribou in every direction. We left the bones in and packed all the meat, except the head. (But we did take the tongues out.) Also took two feet of guts and kidneys. It took us three loads apiece to do it, but we got it done a little after dark. Boiled up two tongues, dry spuds. Drank tea. Hit the sack well satisfied at a day's work.

September 20, 1973
Cloudy, windy

This morning woke but lay in bed till a wolf howled. Then got up and got a fire going. Dave got up then and got water and started making bannock and cut up kidneys while I washed out two feet of caribou guts so to fry. So we had bannock, kidney gravy and fried guts. Good breakfast; didn't get hungry all day.

This morning we hung up the two bulls, then put things in cache, packed and got heading down Comet to Moose Lick cabin. Saw about twenty caribou along the way, also two wolf pups.

Got down to the moose lick expecting to see moose, instead found thirty caribou. So we shot five. We now have enough meat, we might get by. We gutted them, then went to cabin, got fire going. It's dark. Drinking tea, waiting for boiled ribs and dry spuds and glad to have meat.

September 21, 1973
Cloudy, little snow and misting now

Today got up and went right out to caribou. They were safe so went back, had breakfast.

Then went back to the moose lick and made two meat pole caches. Then skinned and cut caribou in half, then hung the ten pieces. It was probably 4:00 p.m. when done. Got back to cabin, fried fat steaks and spuds. Then puttered around while tongues and spuds boil. Also went back to moose lick and hung around there till almost dark. Heard some wolves howling. Kind of damp out, funny weather we're having.

September 22, 1973
Cloudy to mostly cloudy, snow and freezing rain

Again today I got up, went to moose lick to check kills. Nothing. So went back to cabin and had bannock and fried guts for breakfast. Then packed up and went to Main cabin for more 30.06 shells.

Along the way down, I smelled Bull Moose so I know he was close but didn't go after him cuz to far away from any cabins to pack it. When I got to North Fork, there were extremely fresh caribou tracks heading upriver, about 150 in the band. In the three years I been here, I've never seen that before this time of year which is strange.

The beaver pond is deeper than last year at this time. (P.S. Dave went to upper cabin to check on meat.) Anyway got to Main cabin. Everything in order, hooked up stove, got food out of food cache and sleeping bag out of gear cache. Got a fire going. Boiled up some ribs and rice. Now it's dark and I'm comfortable.

September 23, 1973
Mostly cloudy to partly cloudy. It's not getting much above 40°

This morning after breakfast, headed for the upper cabin on Comet. Got 1 ½ miles from Main cabin and ran into a cow moose but somehow I blew it and just creased the shoulder. So I ran in the direction of the cow. Then jumped up on the bank in time to see a bull running towards me. So drilled him two times, watched him go down. Then took off after the cow. Followed it till the blood quit showing. Then just headed to beaver pond, saw a cow swimming across but to my side. So I just watched it. It looked okay so didn't shoot cuz didn't know if it was right one. Went back to bull, gutted it, then hunted cow till noon with no luck. So went up Comet, stopped at Moose Lick cabin, had tea and fried moose guts. Then went on up to get Dave to help pack moose tomorrow.

He's been watching caribou bunch up, he's seen 2,000 today. Some bulls fighting.

September 24, 1973
Clear and freezing; about 10° in morning

Today got up, had bannock and steaks, then watched hundreds of caribou. Then took off for Main cabin and moose. On the way down, stopped and watched two cows and calves thirty yards away. Then went on without incident, got there after dark. Moose o.k. Get to it in morning. This is where it's at for me in life. I know this country. It's my backyard and it's just a small part and every year I'll learn more.

September 25, 1973
Freezing and clouding up

Today got up, had hot cakes and ribs. Then went mile down to moose. Cut him up and packed the hams, rump, back and ribs. Now we're waiting for Swiss steaks, biscuits, gravy, and boiled tongue and rice soup. I think Dave Young will turn out all right in the bush, give or take another year. He's hard working, doesn't bitch much.

September 26, 1973
Clear, windy, then cloudy

This morning I got up, had breakfast. Then we hauled in the last two loads of meat. On the way back I saw the signs of a moose going down as were coming up. But it caught our wind and took off. We wouldn't have shot it though. Got home, had about three pounds of moose and a half loaf of biscuit apiece. Our motto is beginning to be "Eat like pigs, work like slaves." The moose is all packed in though and that's what counts. The loads were about 80 lbs. to 90 lbs. apiece. Three miles round trip each time.

September 27, 1973
Cloudy and warmer

Today we stayed around the cabin, more or less taking it easy. Dave mended his clothes and I washed some of mine. Took a bath. Made a platform for stove so it will be lower in cabin, mainly for heating purposes this winter. Heard a duck quacking tonight. There always seem to be some this late.

Dave will go up Comet to Moose Lick cabin and upper cabin tomorrow.

September 28, 1973
Clear in morning, wind came up N.W., clouds coming this evening.

Today after breakfast, walked down to beaver pond with Dave to start him off. On way down, saw grizzly tracks starting up Eureka, then went on down, stopped at kill but nothing was on it but ravens. Went and saw water splashed on rocks coming out of North Fork making several trails so I knew there were caribou. Got to beaver pond, looked across to see thirty caribou. The bulls are real horny and the cows are still playing hard to get. Several bulls charged each other but no big fight. On the way back a bull caribou walked out of the brush within twenty yards, looked in good shape, but I got meat so just enjoyed watching him. Went to see another just as close. This one with horn broken off. Got home, cut some wood, started making lard, and just puttered round cabin rest of day.

September 29, 1973
Cloud, wind (somewhat) westerly, clearing this evening

Today all I did was hew out two boards for lynx stretchers and plane it smooth. It'll make a good stretcher. Then stacked a bunch of dead spruce boughs for to use as kindling this winter and also cut down a dead tree for firewood. Took a walk. That is it.

September 30, 1973
Clear, not much above freezing in day, freezing hard by night

Not much going today. Fixed window, chinked cabin where it needed it, then cut one-third a cord of dry wood at my wood lot. I already had a cord and a half piled up and usually burn about two cords at this cabin a winter. Came back hour or so before sundown. Fooled around rest of day. Getting bored. I think I'd better move somewhere tomorrow.

October 1, 1973
Rain today, but starting to turn to snow. Snow today at 1,000 ft. higher up

There was a skiff of snow on ground when I got up but melted away. I started going down to mouth of Champion but got to moose kill and it started to rain so came back. No bears have fooled with kill so I think I can go up Comet tomorrow and see how things are going up there. Cooked good size piece rib meat in oven. Turned out damn good but you can taste a slight rut taste. But as mountain man said back in 1830s when he ran into starvin times and had to eat the rotten carcass of a buffalo calf after he chased the wolves off, "Meat's meat in the mountains."

I also put a cover over the meat so as not to get wet. If it gets cold and start freezing like it's supposed to do the meat will be alright. But if it doesn't, I'll have to cut it up into dry meat for winter. Weather ain't actin right!

October 2, 1973
Clear and freezing in morning, clouds came in later in the afternoon

Well got up, had some rice cereal, washed dishes, packed and go off for Moose Lick cabin. The beaver pond is froze over except where beaver has kept it open. Went on up – the snow getting closer to valley floor of Comet as I go up. Three miles up it's about three inches. Got halfway between lower cabin and Moose Lick and came across fresh grizzly tracks; no more than two hours. I think he is heading across Comet toward Champion Creek drainage. Got to Moose Lick, meat is o.k. so just cut off some steaks and took another hide in to cabin to dry. Dave has been here yesterday. Brought my sleeping bag and left note saying caribou meat o.k. at upper cabin too and says the caribou are still around. Also I saw two sets of caribou tracks on way up. The snow is five inches deep here.

October 3, 1973
Cloudy, colder

Got up, had steaks and fried spuds. Then packed what little gear I had to take and walked up to upper cabin. Dave was there. Had some tea and steaks and bannock for lunch. Then walked up Easy Street Ridge to look down Clifford Creek. Saw wolf tracks and caribou tracks. Also saw four caribou. Came back, had boiled ribs and macaroni soup. Then shot the bull before hitting the sack.

October 4, 1973
Hazy to cloudy, not melting much in day

Got up, had steak and biscuits. Packed and went back down to Moose Lick cabin. On the way down saw lots of lynx tracks, good sign for this season. Got there, put in new stove-pipe damper and then put blanket over door all which I got at upper cabin, which is why I went up there.
  Then I cut wood, got a fire going, went over to caribou, got meat and last two hides. Tacked them up on outside wall. Got meat soup going. Now I'm just waiting till it's done.

October 5, 1973
Some snow, cloudy

Got up, didn't do much, cut some trees down and packed them in for wood this winter. Cut some meat. Dave came down. Will head into town tomorrow. I think the meat is safe from bears.

October 6, 1973
Snow, wind

Got up, had meat for breakfast. Then packed and went straight over ridge from Moose Lick to Bear Creek and walked up it to where we usually camp. Along the way we saw a lot of lynx sign, some bear, and marten.

  That breakfast wasn't enough cuz even though we stopped and made tea an hour later we were tired and pretty hungry. So I cut a couple chunks of frozen meat and we wolfed them down. Damn good. We finally got there after dark or rather right at dark. Then I cut down a tree about ten inches through at butt (which is the size you need to see you through evening and in morning cooking, warming up) while Dave made spruce bough beds. Then we sat down, warmed up a little and ate meat soup and tea. Went to bed.

October 7, 1973
Snow, windy, very windy, partly cloudy, very windy!

Today got up at dawn. Got fire going. Made a pot of boiled meat. Ate, packed and took off, heading for road and Eagle. After the first mile, we were tired and hungry which means we didn't sleep long enough and didn't eat enough meat and fat for breakfast. So anyway we got up to head out from there. We had a steep incline, deep drifting snow. The footing was very bad, were falling a good part of time, which drained our strength. We finally made to top to find the wind blowing gusts like gales which benumbed us and made us sleepy but we kept on till we came down to a saddle we had to go through which there was scattered timber. We stopped and got a fire going, had some tea and a bit of meat soup, warmed up and started. Our strength lasted a mile. We came out of the timber to find wind and deep snow again. By the time we were almost to the top of the last hill we were benumbed. Dave's mittens were frozen and torn to ribbons. But on the top we could see where the road was two miles off with just one more hill to climb so we'll make it with rubber legs and empty guts. We made it to that hill, looked down on the road. The moon was shining between the clouds. I looked back across the snow-covered mountains and valleys which was still my home and said, *"Thanks for letting us pass,"* to the mountains and valleys which is who decides who shall pass and who won't.

We got to the road and walked five miles down to Gravel Gulch where the Boone family lived. When we saw snow-covered cabin with lights through the windows, we had quite a good feeling.

We went down to the cabin, introduced ourselves and they had us in. Gave us homemade doughnuts and applesauce, and coffee. After warming up Jack Boone drove us into town. Another day done. Days like this makes one appreciate things much more. I think times like today should happen from time to time to make one appreciate the good things, like a snug cabin with a light inside and smoke drifting from the stovepipe. It would have been easy to say the hell with it and lay down to go to sleep forever. (Back then I didn't know or think about God who holds my life in His hand.)

October 28, 1973
Clear, warm colder

We are now heading back with the dog team and the toboggans we made. Got up and ate breakfast, said good-bye. Then took off for Colorado cabin. The dogs loped most of the way to town, then rest of the way they settled down to a trot. Got to cabin about two p.m. Did the chores. Then Dave came with his dog and little toboggan. I walked the creek to see if there would be any trouble due to creek not froze good enough. But I think we'll make it. Went back and ate.

October 29, 1973
Cloudy, snow, about 25°

Well, I got up at 5:30 a.m., had breakfast, packed and I took off ahead of Dave. We had very good going. There were many open spots but by looking ahead I could gee or haw Ranger, my lead dog, the right way. Around mouth of Utah Creek there was at one time not too long ago a band of ewes and lamb. The first sheep sign on Mission Creek I've seen. Old-timers say they been seen wintering around there. Made it to Clifford Creek cabin by 1 p.m. Could have made to upper cabin on Comet Creek but twelve miles a day for a start with the dogs is enough to get them in shape.

October 30, 1973

Today started off normal – left about 8:15 a.m. Clifford Creek had shelf-ice in it but we got up to the forks by 11:00. Made a fire, had tea and nuts and raisins. Then about 12:00 we took off over the summit and down Easy Street Ridge to Comet Creek and upper cabin. Got there by 3:30. Coming over above timber and at timberline there was moose sign. The dogs even got a scent of one. Everything was as we left it. Caribou hanging okay so no bears came around.

Now I'm just laying here writing this. Just waiting for caribou ribs and bannock with boiled dried apples, brown sugar.

October 31, 1973
Clear, windy, tonight wind stopped, getting colder

Got up late; fooled around till 11:30 a.m. Then slowly packed and hitched dogs and left the upper cabin and Dave and his dog. This is where they shall winter and trap over toward Bear Creek.

We just went down as far as Moose Lick Cabin cuz I wanted to take half a caribou down tomorrow. I didn't have much trouble. Got here o.k. A beautiful sunset tonight. I think it might get cold. But I'm warm and snug, waiting for boiled caribou and macaroni.

November 1, 1973
Clear, temperature dropping to minus 20° at night.

I slept warm and toasty last night on my caribou hide mattress, heavy down quilt. Got up, started a fire, cabin warmed in no time. Had caribou steak and bannock. Then loaded up toboggan and took off. Now I'm on my old trap-line so I rubbed beaver castor on each trap set but won't set traps till Nov. 15. Lynx have already been stopping at sets and rubbing against last year's castor so scent must last long time. Stopped for tea at lower cabin then went on to Main cabin. By the time I hit North Fork, I had broken toboggan handlebar. Then wolf jump out and I missed five times. I was shooting like a greenhorn mainly because I was at my tempers end and wasn't thinking right. I shouldn't have let that happen. Very childish! Then got to cabin to find it minus 20° and bear had been there before hibernating and punched out my window. So then went back to moose and gear cache to find gear scattered below it and moose gone! A hell of a way to end a day.

November 2, 1973
Clear between minus 18° and minus 30° below

After breakfast, cleaned up gear, brought in toboggan to repair. Then followed snowed-over bear tracks till brush got too thick to make it safe. Probably no more than a mile I walked, it going up the hills north of the North Fork. Went back, worked all day on handlebars of toboggan. Cut wood, did chores. Tomorrow Charlie O'Strander should fly over and drop supplies. Then I can start trapping. I've a hundred and one sewing and mending jobs to do.

November 3, 1973
Clear to hazy between minus 10° and minus 30°

Well, O'Strander was supposed to fly over today and drop supplies. So here we sit without dog food and having to wait for drops before we can start moving. I hope he had a good reason! We hauled wood today. Then I spent afternoon repairing toboggan case or bag, moccasins and harnesses and getting anxious to get moving.

November 4, 1973
Same as yesterday

Today just did some mending and chores waiting for O'Strander. He finally came late in afternoon. He dropped some of the fish and all the bait, slab of bacon and a couple of boxes of food, candles, books, traps, etc. I carried them up to cabin. I can start trapping!

November 5, 1973
Same as yesterday

Today I got up, got a fire going, cooked up some cream of wheat cereal, ate and then started getting things organized to load up toboggan for tomorrow's start on my marten line. I'll be gone for five or six days, maybe a week. After I got everything together, I loaded toboggan with ice chisel, axe, and shovel, hitched dogs and took off for beaver pond. Along the way, set a wolf snare then set out the beaver trap. Come back home. Fed dogs, did chores and now it's almost bed time.

November 6, 1973
Clear, cold, but may cloud up tonight or in morning

Today I started day out right with two big bowls of rice cereal and couple cups a tea. Then loaded toboggan, hitched dogs. Then took off, headed for my marten line which starts on a side creek on left side three miles up from cabin. Got there and started up it, setting traps as we go. Didn't have any trouble. Got all the way to Three-forks area of side creek which I named Marten Creek cuz of all the tracks. Got there, set up tent and stove, cut fire wood which took no more than an hour, also chained and fed dogs. Cut wood, started fire, cooked, snug and warm.

November 7, 1973
The same as yesterday

Today I got up a little cold and hurriedly built a fire and the tent was warmed up in a minute. Had breakfast. Then went out, brought in some trees into camp. Then took axe and snowshoes and went up the ridge to pass over to a side creek of Independence Creek, looking it over as a possible trapline. But I think it would be a little hard on dogs and toboggan to make it worthwhile, although a good amount of sign. There's a couple of lines I want to run about on the forks of Marten Creek. But the walk up the ridge was worth it. I could see the country like I was looking at a map. And talk about beautiful.

Also moose signs and caribou have been here. Came back down, ate something, then cut up wood and fixed camp better. Then was dark so fed dogs and came in, put on pot of caribou brisket and split peas. It looks to be colder tonight.

November 8, 1973
Cloudy this morning, clearing by noon

Today I took a dozen traps and walked up the ridge between the middle and north forks of Marten Creek. Took my time and made twelve good sets up to top, making blazes on trees as I go along. When I finished, came back along trail and got halfway down to find a big dark marten. A good way to start the season. Came back, cut wood and fed dogs and fooled around. A good day has passed.

November 9, 1973
Clear, colder, maybe minus 30° to minus 35° tonight

This morning I awoke – probably minus 20° in the tent. Got a fire going in stove and in ten minutes, warm and toasty. Got out of the fart sack and melted snow for tea and cereal. Ate and took off up middle fork of Marten

Creek, setting out seven traps as I went. I walked all the way to upper fork to set last trap. I'd say that this is one of the prettiest side creeks I've laid eyes on, it pushing the fork away above timber, looks like a moose creek. Came back to tent, packed toboggan, hitch dog and came back to Main cabin.

November 10, 1973
Snow, a little warmer, 0°

Today I stayed in cabin and fixed a broken towline on the toboggan, sanded the bottom smooth again and skinned and stretched the marten. Then I hitched dogs and went to beaver pond and checked beaver trap. Nothing there and water all dried up. So pulled trap and went back. I set it for lynx on way, also set another snare. Tomorrow I'll go up Comet and set lynx traps and snares as I go. Also took a much needed bath and changed clothes.

November 11, 1973
Cloudy and warm, clearing, getting colder, wind up high

Today I started off slowly, getting dishes washed, then loaded toboggan, hitched and left. I decided to go to lower cabin today and take my time setting snares and traps and do a good job which I think I did. The dogs worked good and the toboggan held up too. Rough trail, the rabbit population has dropped bad. And I only saw two sets of lynx tracks today but a pack of wolves came through.

I got to lower cabin at dusk. A good day is done.

November 12, 1973
Clear and cold; minus 30°

Left lower cabin at a good early time, setting traps as I go. It's cold work at minus 30°. Almost makes a man want to stop setting. It hurts the hands. Saw a lot of lynx sign and they have really fooled around where I rubbed the beaver castor earlier. Got to Moose Lick, had tea, warmed up, went on up to upper cabin to get meat. Dave is doing o.k. and has really worked on his toboggan. Most of the way I was able to ride.

November 13, 1973
Cold still and at night dropping to -30° or -40°

Today got up at 5:00 a.m. but stayed around, ate caribou and reading till 10 or 11:00. Then Dave and I walked over to the side creek of Bear Creek to break trail to where he will trap. Then came back, showed him how to make a marten set and set a snare. Then it was about dark so came in and now waiting for dog salmon steaks and bannock. Also caribou brisket.

November 14, 1973
Clear and cold

Today got up about 6:30 a.m. and went out and packed up toboggan. Then came back in and had cream of wheat cereal. Then tea, talked for a while with Dave. He is going to take his tent and stove over to Bear Creek today and start his marten line. Then hitched dogs and took off at 9:00. Made good time. Made it to Moose Lick by 10:30, had tea, took down two halves of caribou. Warmed up in cabin. Then left about 12:30, checking traps and snares as I go. Got halfway to find a fair-size lynx with good coloring. I think it will bring about $80. Went on down to lower cabin, got in before dark. Fed dogs, got a fire going. Took dogs inside tonight. All three are as good house dogs as are work dogs.

November 15, 1973
Clear and colder. I believe it's going to be a long winter. HA! Let her rip minus 40°.

Well today was kind of tough on the dogs and little frustrating to me but also a very lucky day. The dogs probably pulled 200 pounds; and still on the level places that didn't have tussocks on it, they could still pull me but I would say it is the very roughest part of the trail. Now for the good part, along the way down I snared a wolf, a small one and black, but a wolf. Then just before we hit North Fork, the dogs' ears and noses pricked up. So stopped and there was a lynx. So killed it, loaded it on sled and went on home. Got a fire going but it took two hours to heat it cuz it's minus 40°. The toboggan held up which is something considering the trail and heavy load. A good day's work is done.

November 16, 1973
Started to get cloudy but cleared, tonight minus 25° to minus 30°

Today just skinned out one lynx and stretched it. The other lynx and wolf are thawing out yet. Be ready in morning. Also listened to a lot of good tapes and did the usual chores.

November 17, 1973
Cloudy and warmer but cleared tonight

About the same as yesterday except skinned out wolf too. Cut meat into steaks and roasts. Hung the rest inside to thaw so I can make hamburger.

In case one wonders how I eat in winter on trapline; well, at Main cabin I eat what normal northerners eat in small, out-of-the-way towns and villages. But when on the trail, I got a tea can that fits into a bigger can or my boiling can. Which whether I'm by a fire camping or in a tent with a woodstove going or in a line cabin, I have boiled meat and rice for dinner and rice cereal in the morning. I can go day after day on this and never get tired or sick. But each night I eat about two pounds of the boiled fat meat, ribs and brisket being the best and fattest.

November 18, 1973
Cloudy bout minus 15° warm spell

Today went down to mouth of Champion Creek re-setting last year's traps as I go. There is a lot of overflow on North Fork that is just froze hard enough for dogs and toboggan. When I got to Champion I set out a wolf set, that place seeming to be a key place. Then came back; distance ten miles round trip, fair amount of lynx sign and rabbits. Got back a couple of hours before dark. Ground up caribou and just fooled around.

November 19, 1973
Clear and cold, minus 30°

This morning I got the meat that is to be sent into the people at the village ready for tomorrow's plane that is to come in with dog salmon and supplies. Then went down North Fork to check for landing place. There's a lot of overflow in places but I think I got one. Then hauled wood in with dogs. Did some much needed sewing and did chores. Cooked up a good pot roast for dinner.

   I heard an owl hooting tonight. The old Indians say it's telling that it's going to warm up. Last year owl wasn't wrong many times.

(Missing Nov. 20 entry)

November 21, 1973
Clear and cold

This morning got up, had hot cakes and bacon. Loaded toboggan went down North Fork, setting traps as I go. It was a little cold minus 30° but went all the way to North Fork Telegraph Station, which is 12 miles down and for the first time I saw fox tracks in the trail.

Set out traps as I went. Still had daylight left so headed back up the trail but dark by time we passed Champion Creek. However, trails hard pack so I'm riding except when I get cold, then I run awhile. Shortly after I passed Champion Creek, I smelled something odd – smoke. I knew Dave was coming down so figured he got to Main cabin. Amazing the smoke drifted that far down (about 5 miles). Well, got home to hear Dave's dog and see light in the cabin. That was nice! A warm cabin and a good friend. A good day.

November 22, 1973
Cloudy and snow, warm at last!

Today we went up to the marten line. Hitched up Dave's dog, too. There was some overflow, we portaged around it. Got to Marten Creek and went up. Caught one on way to tent. We unloaded toboggan, chained dogs. Dave and I walked up middle fork but nothing in traps. Came back. Did chores and now waiting for dinner.

November 23, 1973
Cloudy, snow

Today got up, boiled salmon, eggs and rice. Then I walked the last leg of marten line. Caught one more marten. Set four more traps. Came back to tent. Dave had tea on so drank a cup. Hitched dogs and took off for Main cabin. Dogs ran down Marten Creek, hit Eureka Creek and had knee deep overflow in spots. Portaged around most but went through some which I've broke through to knees in places. But warm weather so didn't worry about dogs or my feet. Got home. Did chores. Cooked up a pot of sow belly and beans and biscuits.

November 24, 1973
Cloudy, clear, cloudy, clear, cloudy, some snow, 0°

I'm lying in my bed looking at my holey long johns, trying to remember what year it was they were white. Think I'd better boil em soon. Took a bath today. Put on clean shirt but ain't got no clean long johns. Cooked for dogs. Skinned and stretched marten. Waited for plane that never showed up.

November 25, 1973
Light cloud or hazy, clear tonight

Got up early today. Had toboggan in last night to ice off. Took it out this morning. Came in, had a batch of hot cakes and hot tea. Then loaded toboggan and took off, heading up Comet. There was five inches of snow on the trail but dogs were still able to pull me most places. Got about to lower cabin and saw a trap drug off but new snow made it a little hard to follow trail. But at the end of it was a dandy lynx cat so knocked his noggin and loaded it on, then re-set trap. Went on past four traps and two snares to find another in trap. So now have another $180 to $200 with the two lynx. Then on to Moose Lick cabin without any more. Got there, did chores, had some tea, puttered around. Then cooked supper. A very worthwhile day.

November 26, 1973
Cloudy, warm light snow

Today woke as usual. Got a fire going. Cooked up some rice, then fried it in moose grease. Went to cached caribou, dropped down a back half of caribou. Took it back to cabin to load on toboggan, hitched dogs and left the trail packed. We had little trouble. I rode most of the way. Got to beaver pond, saw Dave's tracks. Got on North Fork, saw him so came back up with us. It probably wasn't later than 2 p.m. Made good time and had a very enjoyable two days. This is beginning to be a very comfortable trapline and through some mighty fine country.

November 27, 1973
Light clouds, windy from the north

It was beginning to just get light when I woke up. Got a fire going. When it warmed up, Dave made some biscuits and cooked up some steaks while I loaded toboggan. Ate breakfast. Then hitched and got headed down North Fork to Telegraph Station, fixing sets and making new ones. On the way down, about three miles, saw the marks of a trap drug off. Looked up a ways to see a large lynx cat. So clubbed it and drug him and trap to toboggan, loaded him and re-set trap. Went on. Got to wolf set to find wolves had been there. Pissed all over set, ate the chopped up meat, all except under trap. So re-set trap and scattered meat and hope for better luck next time.

November 28, 1973
Cloudy to clearing

Today came back home setting six more traps for fox and lynx. It will be interesting to see if I catch a fox there, tricky as wolves it seems. Good trail, now packed down hard as rocks. When got home, did chores, fooled around. This finishes first total run of 25 mile line. Caught two marten and three lynx cats.

November 29, 1973
Cloudy to clearing

Got up before daylight to get Dave going early. Ate breakfast. Then he took off and I'm glad. Guess I like people in towns but not out here for much more than overnight.

Skinned out two lynx and put them on stretchers. Did chores. Plan on staying around camp till 2nd of December.

November 30, December 1, 2, 3, 4, 1973
Cold, between minus 40° and minus 50°

Worked around cabin. Did chores. Stretched fur. Cooked for dogs. Washed clothes. Read a lot and thought a lot. It's the 4th now, same thing except took a walk to the beaver pond. That's what a cold spell is. Time to look at yourself and see if you are fighting the country or living with it.

December 5, 1973
Cloudy to almost clear, then cloudy and tonight snow

Well, today looks like time to move so went up Eureka to Marten Creek. Got to tent without any marten caught. Sawed up some wood, chained and fed dogs. Then walked up middle fork to upper fork, checking and setting three traps. Caught one fair-sized marten. Picked him up on way back to tent. Stopped on way to pick up a dry tree. Took it back to tent. Got a fire going. Sawed up and split wood. Got snow melting for water. Then it was about dark so now just lay around in snug, warm tent.

December 6, 1973
Cloudy & windy, warmer

Woke before first light. Fried up bacon and some bannock. Took off with snowshoes to run last side line. I should have caught three marten. Somehow they missed the traps. But got to the fourth from last to find a marten. Went on back to tent, hitched dogs. Took off for Main cabin. Got there about 1:30 or 2:00. So this trip, I've caught two more marten.

December 7, 1973
Cloudy little wind, clearing in afternoon

Today went down North Fork line. I decided to make a round trip out of it cuz short on dog feed and so got to hustle so can run into town. Got to where I caught a lynx last run down to find one again! Killed it and went on. Got about 8 miles down to find a #4 trap drug off. So followed the wind-blown-over trail and every time it went through willow patch, it looked like a D8 cat. Went through. I knew it was a wolf so went back for 30.06. Lost the trail for a while then by chance only happen on it again. Finally found him. Took a bead on his neck from 40 yards and ended the life of a worthy foe. It was with mixed feeling when I stood over him. He almost made it – toe almost pulled off. And if I would've missed his trail, he would have won. But he would have killed as viciously and did. In the wild, we're all part of the game.

December 8, 1973
Clear and cold, tonight high, scattered clouds, moon is out

Today was skinning day. Skinned and stretched two marten and lynx. Just skinned wolf. Rolled him up and put him on roof with other wolf. It just turned dark when I finished wolf. Between skinning and stretching and doing chores, it took most of the daylight hours. It was a beautiful sunrise today, although the sun never came above the hill in the southeast. That wolf is very big, weight over 100 pounds.

December 9, 1973
Cloudy

Today just fooled around, did chores. Took lynx off stretcher. Then loaded fur and meat to take to town.

December 10, 1973
Cloudy, almost fog, warm. Distance traveled 11 miles

Today got up well before daylight. Got a fire going, put tea water and wash water on. Then jumped into bag till cabin warmed and wash water hot. Got dressed. Made tea. Put on a couple strips of bacon. Then hot cakes. Ate. Put things away. Hitched dogs and headed up Comet and on to town. It didn't light up till a mile up Comet. But before that, I caught a lynx at beaver pond. So was happy as a coon. But this made top-heavy load even more so and there was several inches of snow and overflow at each crossing, which is slow going. Got eight miles up to find another lynx which made it even more top heavy. Got to Moose Lick cabin, had tea and a bannock. Dogs rested. Then went up to Dave's place (upper cabin). Got there after dark. Had no trouble. Just didn't get to read much today.

December 11, 1973
Clear then cloudy, snow

Today, Dave and I went toward head of Comet looking for moose. Dave said I could take back two halves of caribou if I wanted to run my line through once more which I will do. We didn't see any moose but know they are around. But we did get to go through some of the prettiest timber line country there is. Got back well after dark.

December 12, 1973
Cloudy

Today took my time, loaded toboggan and fooled around. Then finally left for Moose Lick cabin. We didn't have much load cuz left fur and meat with Dave. Took off and dogs felt good and made good time and I rode most of the way. Got to where caribou was hanging, across from cabin to find Dave's dog broke loose and followed me. So took him to cabin and chained him up, did chores, went over and got meat.

Brought it back. Fed dogs. Was sawing wood when Dave came. He'll spend the night and take dog back tomorrow.

December 13, 1973
Cloudy

Today got up. Got a fire going. Cooked. Washed dishes and loaded and took off to Main cabin. Along the way, re-setting sets and made two more. Didn't catch any in the last couple days. Got to Main cabin in five hours. I brought along Dave's clock to time how long it would take. Could make it faster when not stopping at every set. Distance 11 miles.

December 14, 1973
Clear minus 20°, cloudy tonight 0°

Today decided to make a round trip out of it and go down North Fork. This time springing traps. I was hoping to pick up a lynx or two going down and I should have but two lynx were lucky. One walked through two snares without disturbing them which disturbs me. So fix them (sprung traps cuz will be going to town) and then dogs and I went on. We went through overflow in several spots. Got my moccasins wet but made trip o.k. Foxes have been out but still outsmarting me. Got to a lynx set to find a lynx had went there but missed stepping on trap. I got skunked today.

December 15, 1973
Cloudy, snow

Today had the dogs haul in the pile of wood, it took seven loads but will have a good start for when I come back after holiday. Then put dogs back. Got five snares and three traps to set out a side line for lynx. These sets and snares I shall leave out over holidays. I fastened them to trees instead of drags so there won't be any snowed-over trails to follow.

December 16, 1973
Warm, cloudy

Stayed around cabin today. Fix harnesses, toboggan and moccasins. Then loaded toboggan. Tomorrow I'll head up Comet and to town. Cooked up some steaks for supper and went to bed. Read till sleepy.

December 17, 1973
Warmer, cloudy

Got up early. Had hot cakes. Then took off up Comet. Didn't catch any lynx below lower cabin. But next trap had a large lynx cat so knocked him off, loaded him. Went past next and nothing. Then next three traps all had large lynx cats. By then I had a fair-sized load in toboggan. I sprung all traps but three because I'll be in town too long and they'll get covered by snow. Dave came to Moose Lick to get caribou and I caught up with him before too long and we went on up to upper cabin. Then we skinned out all four lynx so didn't get to bed till 11:00 or so. Go to Clifford tomorrow.

December 18, 1973
Cloudy, windy, warm, little snow

We left upper cabin early and started over Easy Street Ridge. We hitched all four to my toboggan, then tied Dave's onto mine. Then took turns breaking trail and working toboggans over the drifted snow. Then when we got over the top and back toward timber, Dave hitched his dog to his sled and went on in to Clifford cabin that way. The weather was warm and there was much overflow but had little trouble at all. Got a fire going, did chores and so on.

December 19, 1973
Above freezing! South wind, cloudy

Left well before light. There was an average of eight inches of water most of the way, but it is warm so no trouble. Got to Seventymile Trail by 1:00 p.m. and went on into town. Everybody welcomed us. We found the cabin in good shape. Glad to be here.

Two fur buyers looked at my furs. The first one wouldn't give any more than $1,125 at first, then finally went to $1,150 but that wasn't good. I have 12 lynx, 5 marten and 2 wolves. Jess Knight looked at them and would give me $1,185 for them. I told him I wanted

$1,200. He took it. So I won't be going back to trapline till Jan. 20th and stay until about April 1st. This is the last journal.

February 22, 1974

Today's a hang around the cabin day. The last couple a days was a blizzard. The first I've seen on the North Fork proper. I had to run my traps in it cuz if I caught any fur during the blow the drag trail would be blown over. Fortunately this is a period when the lynx are up high, not in the valleys but still I lost one trap and drag cuz of blow. Ya win some, ya loose some. I do, however, by now have between $350 to $400 and over a month to go.

I got a moose last Sunday, the 17th. It's an interesting story in itself. I and the dogs were on our way up North Fork to Slate Creek where I want to extend my line to for next year. It's mainly a marten country and though I was planning to set some traps, I did want fall and blaze cabin logs for next summer. Well I got side tracked a little. I was about three miles up North Fork when the dogs behind (I was breaking trail) who were a fair piece back before (cuz toboggan was heavily loaded) – were now on my heels sniffing the air, ears perked up. So I stopped and looked at the dogs and said to them, "*Okay, if you want me to, I'll shoot it.*" Though I hadn't seen what it was. Went back to toboggan and got 30.06, walk on a little ways, looked to my left to see a moose walk across a sloping tussock field about a hundred yards. So shot but the gun misfired, tried the same shell again, same thing. Ejected it and tried another shell. That one worked. The bull took about eight steps and fell over dead. Heart shot. How's that for shooting? I was very low on meat but not no more!

I'll continue tonight. I got to finish my lunch (roasted boudins and dried mixed fruit pie and hot) so I can go cut some more wood in my wood lot.

It took us two days to haul it all in. In loads the first day brought in 2/3rds of the meat and the next day went back and loaded rest in toboggan and set wolf and marten traps and snare around kill. Then brought the load home. The weather the day I shot the moose was clear and minus 20° but clouds came and it warmed up to minus 11° so it was comfortable weather to work in. But today the sun is high enough to warm the day considerably. For instance: awoke this morning it was minus 30° but this afternoon it was 12° above so you can see what a difference the sun makes. I'll add to this letter ever once in a while.

Well, it's the third of March now. I ran through my trapline. Fur is still coming in slowly. The lynx are just coming down. I caught one medium, two large, and saw tracks of two others. So maybe next trip they will be down. I only caught four more marten. I sprung the marten line that I trapped the most as to leave a good amount of marten for next year. I did however catch 17 on that six-mile line which in this country is good. 20 mile is normal. I went over this but don't think any more than the surplus.

Well, I'm in Eagle now. Had a very good trip in weather very warm and sunny and trail good. Went to upper cabin first day and next made it all the way into Eagle in 9 hours. It's between 30 and 35 miles in from upper cabin. I'm staying in here for about 4 – 5 days then go back out to run traps and maybe a little work on cache.

This year ended with 20 lynx, 17 marten, 2 wolves, 2 fox. Total miles of line: 24. I made about $2,100 that season, which for a bachelor trapper like me in 1973 was enough to get through to another winter and with a good grubstake for the next. That was all I really cared about.

Last Season on the Trapline

Introduction

Since white men came to America there's always been those who want to go out past the edge of the frontier – the "Mountain Man." Every generation till the Lord comes again will have these renegades of civilization. Well, I was one of those renegades who got blessed with fulfilling that desire.

I went to Alaska in 1968, June 5th, 10 a.m., a day after graduation from high school. I was 17-years-old. In my 21 years of living in the Alaskan bush I have been fortunate enough to do a variety of occupations. I've worked on commercial fishing boats, worked for Alaska Fish and Game, worked as a horseback guide and transporter for hunters, worked on the Alaska Pipeline, and fought forest fires, as well as run the trapline with my dogs for nine years.

When I moved to where I was to call home in 1971 I lived in an Indian village on the banks of the Yukon River when I wasn't on the trapline. From this village I married my wife in 1975. We have a son and a daughter, all of whom have traveled the mountains and rivers of our part of Alaska with me the old-fashioned way – dogs, on foot, or with horses.

We trapped this country from 1971 to 1979 about a decade, long enough to go through a complete cycle of the fur critters running around that country. I'll explain a little that might help ya understand some things ya might have wondered about. When I first went out there in '71 I'd already did a little trapping in southeast Alaska on those islands on the coast, as well as over northeast of Talkeetna. I'd wintered there taking care of a guide's horse string though the winter of '70 - '71. Well I got to Eagle with three horses to help me get some of my outfit to where I was gonna trap. Then had a guy who had a truck there in Eagle help me get those horses back to Palmer. I sold them there.

Anyway that first winter of '71 - '72, I made some dumb mistakes and ended up having to take a job back in the spring working a fish wire for Alaska Fish and Game down near Petersburg. Then I went back up to begin again trying to make a go of it trapping. There really weren't much marten those first three years; mainly snowshoe rabbits and lynx. Oh I caught a few marten in that winter, maybe 27 or 28 but lynx were chasing the rabbits and coming to beaver castor lures which are a sex stimulant. They'd come to it easily so for the first three years like I said it was lynx.

In winter of '74 - '75 it snowed early just as the creeks were freezing. I'm talking waist deep snow by mid-November. Going out with the dog team up Mission Creek to get to the pass I had to go over to get to my trapline was a "canyon" creek which was very near impossible to get over. The creek is fairly deep in many places and as I said the snow was to my waist. I had to break the trail using snowshoes up and back to smash it down and then let it freeze overnight. That's called breaking out the trail – necessary so the dogs wouldn't flounder. Also the creek would cave in cuz the ice was so thin. I'd take a ten-foot-pole and hold onto the end of it then kinda throw it out where the ice looked bad. Just that pole end hitting on top of the snow would make it cave in. I'd have to whack out a portage around the spot then get back on that creek. It was slow, slow going. So slow to where I had to go back to Eagle and get some more grub.

Fifty miles took me nineteen days to get to the Main cabin on Eureka Creek. Then the guy who was to drop my dog salmon for the dogs never did. So I set rabbit snare but the rabbits were dying off along with the lynx. I finally got a moose as I was heading back to town for dog feed. I turned around and stayed out there a while but the lynx weren't interested in the castor anymore. They stopped breeding when the rabbits died off. So I finally decided to call that season quits.

The building of the Trans-Alaska Pipeline was going on and I went to Fairbanks on the mail plane and joined the Laborers Union. I had to wait till April before my number came up out of the hall to go to work. So I bounced at a bar on Second Street. Not a job I'd recommend especially during the pipeline days but I survived. Got up there on the pipeline and made enough to get an old international pickup, a chain saw, and some grub money. One more thing – I got married.

Now I needed to build a cabin near the village where my wife's people are from. Her dad let us build on his Native allotment right on the banks of the Yukon about a mile upriver from the village. We went out to the trapline and made meat that fall of '75 then I went up on the pipeline again for a month then back out to the trapline. Well there wasn't any lynx or rabbits or many marten but I fooled around and figured out how to outsmart the foxes that were hard to catch. Got a few and a wolverine. Still it was starvin times in the fur department so I went back in the spring to the pipeline for a month. I fought forest fires some in the summer of '76, and the winter of '76 - '77 was the same.

Around then was the time Jimmy Carter thought he was doing us a big favor by making a huge amount of Alaska bush into National parks. Well one was west of my country and me and another guy and our dogs were hired to take a government fella out on west of me up Ruby Creek to the headwaters of Charley River (not to be confused with Charlie Creek which was on the north side of Yukon). I made some money off them. Adeline was pregnant with our little girl (she did walk out there to the Main cabin behind the dogs when she was 5-months on).

Well went out one more time on the pipeline that spring. By then the pipeline was running oil and I had had enough of that work anyway. So in the winter of '77 - '78 my wife stayed in town, Jody being newborn in July of '77, and I went to the trapline. I knew there wasn't any lynx but hoped marten had come back and they had. Set out the traps up Mission Creek (it froze good that year) and on over Easy Street (the pass between Comet and Clifford which is part of Mission Creek) to Comet Creek and on down to North Fork and up to the Main cabin on Eureka Creek.

The marten seemed to be everywhere and after staying at the cabin for a couple days went back to town and picked up nine marten. I ran the line two more times and got 54 marten even with a wolverine stealing nine or ten. I never caught that rascal. Noticed he had a toe missing. Once they've been caught in a trap and get away they become trap savvy.

In 1978 I took my family out to the trapline. It was a warm snowy winter. We stayed till Christmas and did all right even though the traps were plugged up with snow much of the time. I cut cord wood after trapping season and fought fires in the summer. Then come the last year on trapline which you'll read about shortly. So in ten years you can see the cycle of the fur critters. They're up and down.

We quit the trapline in 1980, started a Sawmill and farmed using horses for power. I logged and packed hunters into the mountains with the horses till we decided to do something different. We loaded up the stock truck with gear and horses and belongings and moved to Wyoming. There we logged, rode horseback around the mountains, and of course hunt elk and fished for trout.

But this story is about the best season we had on the trapline. It was also the last one for me. The year was

1979. I was 29 and by now was at the age where I was beginning to have a little sense. My wife was about the same age, our son 8, and our daughter 2. Along with our four sled dogs, we begin this story.

I should add that we had some help along the way. At one point a couple of young men from the village, Danny David and Billy Silas, walked out to the trapline with us to see the country and help us pack in the airdropped outfit to our cache. Then they walked back. You'd think boys who'd grown up in Eagle Village would know all about the bush but their generation didn't go very far from home. They didn't trap, just fought fire some. It was their elders, those who had come of age before WWII, that knew how to live in the bush so it was good they came with us. They were enjoyable and helpful on the trail.

This story is dedicated to renegades like me. I hope you find it enjoyable and maybe helpful. May God have mercy on your souls and lead you to the Lord Jesus Christ.

Gearing Up for the Trapline

For us the trapping season starts along the banks of the Yukon River, even though our trapline is 50 miles out in the mountains, because our sled dogs have to eat and the cheapest source of dog food is that which the Lord put in the river – dog salmon. There's a large run of these fish that come up the Yukon every fall heading on up to their spawning grounds in the headwaters of the Yukon River in Canada. And so, with a couple of 60-

foot gillnets placed in eddies along the bank of the river you'll catch your supply of dog food. I usually figured 125 salmon per dog. Since I ran a four dog team 500 dog salmon would do the job.

I'd set the nets the last couple days of August and try to be done fishing by the 13th or 14th of September. The salmon run would start slow, but by the 8th or 10th of September I'd be catching 50 to 80 a day or more. I'd split, hang, and semi-dry the salmon we'd caught till the 10th then I'd leave the rest of what I caught whole. It's cool enough by the 10th of September that the flies pretty much stop buzzing around.

A typical day begins at 6:30 a.m. and after coffee and such I'd be in my boat heading to my nets. It would take about two hours to pick both nets and get back home. I'd usually leave the catch in the boat and go have breakfast then go down and cut and hang fish which took another hour or two depending on how good the catch was.

The rest of the day would be spent repairing gear or getting airdrops ready. Airdrops are our food and necessary items for the trapline. We pack them in burlap bags and wrap them with strapping tape till they are rock hard. Any part that is loose will explode on impact. The airdrops are dropped out of a low, slow flying airplane at a prearranged time and spot. This way you don't have to build an airstrip, which is good because you'll have enough trouble with bears tearing your place up without having to worry about someone flying in and taking things. The dried and whole salmon are just tied into loose bundles and thrown out of the plane without much trouble. (See appendix for grub list for four months.)

Dog Packing Out to Trapline
We always try to leave on the 16th of September figuring a week to get to the Main cabin on the trapline. (Main cabin is where we base out of for trapping.)

Our system is simple. We pack our food, tarp or a piece of plastic, cook gear, and my sleeping bag on our dogs. My wife and son would each carry their sleeping bags and change of clothes on a pack-board that wouldn't be more than 15 lbs. which they could handle. I'd pack our daughter, who was then two years old, on my back.

Day One
The first day leaving the village I'd have our nephew drive us out on a gravel road about 17 miles into the mountains to our summer-fall trail. Heading out from there it was only 37 miles to our main trapline cabin, but it's pretty hard going compared to mountains in the western USA. The footing is often spongy and rough or brushy, or steep and rocky. Because of the difficulty for my wife and kids, six miles is a good day.

As we'd get to the trailhead (there's no trail really, it's just where we start from) we'd unload dogs, gear, and family. Getting started with the dogs is the hard part. They want to explore everything but somehow we get them packed and started off. This is bear country, grizzlies in particular, so we've got our rifles ready at all times. Our boy carries our .22 and shoots Ptarmigan, a medium-sized game bird, as we go for added meat.

The travel would be slow. We'd stop a lot but the day was beautiful, mountains still would have some colors left, and one would feel good to be underway with no real time pressures on us. We'd have ten days till the airdrops at Main cabin are due so there's no rush.

We'd make six mile camp about 3:30 p.m. It's on an open bench above a brush creek right at the timberline so the view is good. There's enough dry wood for a fire, water not too far away, poles to make a frame to put the tarp on for a lean-to. It's 4:30 or 5:00 p.m. and Mom gets supper going over the fire. The kids are playing, the dogs are chained, each eating a half a dried dog salmon, and me, I'm on my back, cup of tea in hand, enjoying the good life. Supper on the trail, before we get meat, is usually macaroni and cheese. It's easy and stays with you and if we get any Ptarmigan we fry them on the side. Other than crawling into sleeping bags in our lean-to the day is done.

Day Two

The day would start out nice and frosty. I would get a fire going and put on the coffee pot which had a layer of ice on it. The fire sure felt good. We aren't in a rush to break camp cuz the frost on the brush would get our pants wet. I cook breakfast – boil a pot of rice and raisins, put some dried milk, butter, and sugar in it – get the kids and wife up. We would eat and then take our time breaking camp and packing dogs. Then we're off. The brush is still a little wet but not bad.

We climb uphill all morning. The first half of the climb would be spongy with poor footing then it would kind of top out before the next leg. As we'd head down to the creek, we'd see clouds coming. By tonight it might snow some. We'd get down to a creek and follow it for several miles till we'd decide to camp. Our daughter was a good little traveler, not complaining, just sitting in her little pack-board seat looking around. The dogs did good and didn't run off. We didn't see any game today. We made camp down a ways on the creek. Got camp set up, fire going, dogs fed and bedded down, put extra wood under the lean-to cuz it looked like it could get wet, and built fire close to it. It's raining now but feels like it could turn to snow. May as well eat supper and get into our bags and read a western.

Day Three
Woke up to snow and it's still coming down. We had a good camp so instead of getting wet and getting our daughter cold we'd lay over a day and see if it gets any better. Kept fire going and read westerns, drank a lot of tea, and played with the kids. Maybe it's not a bad day.

Day Four
We woke up to snow on the ground and partly cloudy skies. Best get going so we broke camp, packed the dogs, and put on the "big skedaddle." We have eight

miles to go but my line cabin closest to town (about 35 winter-trail miles from town) is there waiting with wood split and ready for firing up the stove. We have a long climb and lots of brush to go through until we start the last two miles down to the cabin. Since there's four inches of wet snow on top of that – we'd best get started. Everyone, dogs too, seem to be holding up o.k. We stop a lot but as we start the last two miles to the cabin, our daughter starts crying. Her feet are cold. I cut my wool jacket under my arms, take off her rubber boots, and stick her feet inside my jacket. This helped but she was still uncomfortable and still cried a little. We saw some caribou but didn't want to shoot any till we'd get to the Main cabin.

Finally, we came to the bluff above Comet Creek and see the cabin across it over yonder saying, "come on in." The cabin hadn't been hit by bears this time. We always took everything out of the cabin and put it in the cache, then left the door open. I'd find when I'd close the door if a bear would come by the pesky varmint would get mad and tear things up. When the door would be left open he didn't do the same amount of damage.

At last we'd get to the cabin and get a fire going. These little line cabins warm up fast and so does our daughter. The cabin is 9 feet by 9 feet and has a bunk the full length of the back wall. There are shelves and a small table against one side, and the stove and wires for drying wet clothes is on the other side. There are two small windows, one on each side, a split-pole roof with sod on it, and a dirt floor. When you would come in cold, wet, tired, and hungry enough to eat a wolverine hide and all, you see the shack like a Hilton hotel! Anyway, we make it to the town end of the trapline and feel like we're home. By the way, the bunk is made up of poles with wild hay cut and laid on them with canvas tacked over the hay. The bunk is three feet off the floor. You'll see why when it's 40 below.

Day Five
We stayed at the cabin this day. I wanted to get in some wood for the season, needed to pull the toboggan down off the cache for the coming winter season, and there were a few odds and ends that needed doing. Always liked this place. It has a rocky mountain in back of the cabin with sheep on it and high ridges that reach well above the timberline. This is caribou country with good winter moose range as well as sheep on the ridges.

Day Six
We'd eat another hearty breakfast of rice and raisins, load up, and head out. The snow was gone. We're following our trapline trail down this creek valley. It's a fairly broad valley and the trail is over usually hard ground so the going is good. We're going to stop at a cabin we built. We call it the "Moose Lick Cabin" because it sits across the creek from the moose lick. If a guy has patience he can get a moose here and sometimes caribou. You just sit on it and wait. It's a mineral lick and they paw at the dirt and lick it. It's only six

miles to this cabin so it's a short day which is good cuz I wanted to get some wood laid up for this winter and do whatever else was needed.

There are a lot of spruce hens along the way so my boy shot a mess for dinner. My wife cooked up bannock bread, fried up the birds, and made gravy. Got us a good feed tonight. This cabin is about the same as the last one.

Day Seven

Last day! But a long one for the family – 11 miles to the Main cabin and HOME for the next three months. As we got to the mouth of the creek where it empties into the North Fork of Fortymile River we found the water is bank to bank today so instead of crossing at riffles and walking gravel bars we have to walk the last two miles in the brush. Finally we go up to where we can cross (I'd wear hip boots this time of year cuz one is always crossing creeks and rivers) and I'd carry my son across first, then daughter, then Mom. The dogs wade across and then it's a short walk to the cabin. We found a bear had been there – it was a mess! It took an hour or two to clean up the mess and get things down from the cache. Got a fire going in the stove and Mom fried up another bannock bread, cooked the spruce hens our son shot, and made gravy. A good way to end a day. Stars would be out tonight. Got to start the hunt tomorrow. There was a lot of fresh moose sign along the river. I fell asleep thinking about making meat.

The Fall Season on Trapline

Got up, the eastern sky was just getting gray, and headed down the river to the mouth of the creek we followed before. There's a beaver pond there which had a lot of moose sign around it. Got down to the beaver pond and found a place to stand with a good view of the area and waited. I didn't see any new sign from the day before of them moving around. Sometimes the bulls will come down the first half of September, get the cows, and go back up the mountain with them so they're only in the valley a few days. Other years they are around most of the fall. I waited around till 9 a.m. then walked up river and back home hunting as I went.

Got home, the kids and wife were up and had breakfast ready and I brought my appetite so ate and sat over a cup of coffee awhile. Then my boy and I went down to a place where there's a lot of standing dead trees (the wood lot). We spent the afternoon cutting cord wood – chopping down, limbing, and bucking them in six foot lengths with a swede saw and then stacking the wood. When the snow comes we can haul them on the toboggan with the dogs. We went back to the cabin to find some tea and biscuits there. Sure tasted good.

Sat around for an hour or so then decided to hunt awhile. Went up the creek the cabin is on. Was about a mile up when I heard something strange to my left on the side of the hill. I stopped for a while, didn't see anything so started on and suddenly heard a crashing of brush. Looking, I saw two young bull caribou cutting across in front of me about 50 yards off. I threw my gun to my shoulder, aimed, and fired at the bull in the lead. He stopped and so did the other. I aimed at the one in the rear and fired and it fell. I aimed to shoot the first again but he was down already. We were "making meat."

I knew we wouldn't have time to get them home tonight so I gutted them, spread-eagled them, took the tongues and kidneys, and headed home. The kids and Mom heard the shots and were looking for me when I came home. When I handed Mom the tongues and kidneys she got a sparkle in her eyes cuz she, like all good Indians or mountain men know, life without meat is just "starvin times." Now on to the good life – tongue soup and kidney gravy. Next to roasted caribou head, these are top of the list of "fit food."

The next morning after a good breakfast of kidney gravy and fry bread, the dogs, my son, and I went up the creek, cut up the caribou and packed it back down to the cabin. A dog can pack two hind legs each or two shoulders and a rump. I packed ribs, neck, and such. We got back home by early afternoon. We've enough meat to get us by a month or so. Getting this meat right away will take some of the pressure off. However, we must keep hunting to get a moose or more caribou. Without meat we'd run out of the staples that were to be air-dropped. The plane will be coming tomorrow Lord willing.

We heard the plane engine about 10 a.m. then saw the plane coming over the ridge across the creek so ran back of the cabin to an open tussock flat where we had pre-arranged for the plane to drop the supplies. As I got back there the plane was dropping the first pass. Three bundles were dropped. This kept up until the plane, a 180 Cessna, was empty of cargo for us. Then we'd go out and gather up our supplies and put them on the cabin edge of the flat. Then with backboards we'd carry them to the cache a couple hundred yards away. Some things would go directly to the cabin, like dried apples for an apple pie.

We didn't quite get done packing when the last plane load came in. This was mainly fish for the dogs and one 50 lb. bag of dog food to cook with whole fish. It took us the rest of the day to pack the airdropped bags off the flat to where they were to go. By then, we were hungry. Mom had supper ready for us and we were ready to clean it up. She had some fried tenderloins and gravy, fried potatoes (from dried potatoes), homemade bread, an apple pie, and of course lots of tea. Laid around and read a western and listened to the battery-operated radio till bed time.

The rest of the time was spent getting wood cut, things in shape for the coming trapping season, and hunting for a moose. Also, this year was a blueberry year. The kids and Mom would get gallons of them in a short time and make blueberry jam and syrup for pancakes. Life is good.

As September closed and October came in I wondered if the moose would ever come back down to the valley. I kept hunting though and one day by the beaver pond I smelled a bull moose in rut. I wasn't too excited about shooting a bull in full rut. There's no fat on them and the meat tastes awful. Anyway, take what you can get and be glad of it. So I started around the corner of the beaver pond and what do you know – a barren cow was across the other side of the beaver pond just a looking at me. Well, there was meat and I best dispatch it so I did. Walked over the beaver dam to the moose, it was partly in the water still, but it was no problem gutting it. That was one fat moose. We'd be able to make lard which we were in need of plus all the meat we needed.

After I spread-eagled the moose so it wouldn't sour, I took one fat-encased kidney (about the size of a football) and went home. Mom and kids were happy enough to dance a jig. I guess I was too and I bet you can figure out what we ate that night.

Next morning we all went down to the beaver pond to cut up and cache moose meat. Still haven't seen any fresh bear sign. Maybe we won't have any bear troubles. Anyway, we cut up the moose and moved pieces into the trees where we'd put the cache and cut poles to make a ladder. Then took some heavy gauge wire we'd brought along and with wire in hand climbed up ladder leaning on the tree all the way to the top, tied and nailed wire on one tree then the other tree. Cache built, we stopped and fried up some meat. After eating and drinking some hot tea and letting out a hearty belch, I tied a piece of lighter wire on the eight pieces of meat, then with a long rope we hoisted a piece at a time by throwing one end of the rope over the wire. Then we'd all grab that end and pull up the meat. Mom and Son would hold it and I'd put the ladder up against the wire weighted down by the meat, climb up, and tie the meat to the wire. We'd do this time and again until all the meat was hung. The lowest point of the hanging meat is a good thirteen feet from the ground and at least five feet from both trees. This meat cache turned out to be a good one. It was safe from the bears – we didn't lose any meat. Later, when the river froze, we'd come down with toboggan and dog team and haul it home.

It's the 6th or 7th of October and things are freezing and by the 15th it's below zero. Everything is pretty much froze up. However, this year a freakish thing happened. Winds came from the south and things warmed up. There was a miniature break-up and this warm spell lasted about ten days. It was strange because once winter comes here it stays, but this year it didn't. During this nice weather the kids played outside all day wearing only a light jacket. We've got most everything ready for the trapping season so we just putter around. Mom tanned a beaver hide and made me a beautiful pair of trail mittens.

Let me tell you, my wife Adeline was and is a blessing to me. Back then I took a lot of things for granted but looking back after forty-three years of marriage I couldn't have picked a better wife. For starters, she really loved me and secondly, she'd follow me when I'd say this is what we're gonna do. She'd set her mind to do the best job she could. She's lived in conditions that many a woman would have left their husbands for, but not her. She basically said, *"Where you go, I go and your people will be my people,"* whether we went to Wyoming, or Mongolia, or out on the trapline. She pitched right in.

I'd have to leave her and the kids for three or four days by themselves but she'd tough it out. She made all our winter moccasins, my moose hide parka, and the beaver skin mitts I mentioned earlier, with Indian-tanned moose hide on the palm and a heavy wool blanket liner. That hide was tough and pushing a skin needle through was hard work let alone tanning that beaver hide. But she made them and I used them for years, then my son used them. I never got cold in them like I did in store-bought mitts even at 60 below. Not many women like that. I am blessed. She's 72 now goin on 52. Not bad lookin either!

The Trapping Season Begins

Around the first of November it cooled off. Some things froze up again. I've been cutting dry salmon up into 2x4 inch pieces for bait in my traps. I put a light wire through the meat and attach it to the poles on marten sets. Dry fish seems to be the most practical bait to use. It brings them in.

The long trapline, back up the creek we walked down, will have to be the last one set because there's not enough snow to have the dogs pull the toboggan down nor are the creeks froze good enough. There should have been snow aplenty by now and everything frozen up by mid-October, but like I said, this was a freak year. Anyway, I decided to set the line out that the Main cabin is on. It's only eight miles long and I could set it out in a couple of days. Unfortunately, in the country I was trapping in, I couldn't figure how to make loops of my lines. Between the creeks the country was pretty rough. So we always had to double back. I'd set this line first and carry what I needed in a backboard.

Most of the poles and traps were out but the lower end of the line had to be rerouted by way of where we shot the two caribou and then stay on that side of the creek for another mile. A single bit axe is the trapper's main tool. The trail axe with a two foot handle is what I prefer. I keep it sharp with a file. You'll need it to cut brush and such out of where you want the trail to go, you'll need it to blaze your trail, and of course to make your different trap sets.

The first line to set out goes up the creek the cabin is on for four miles and then goes up a side creek I named Marten Creek, for another four miles. What with rerouting the line farther off the creek and making new sets, I only went as far as the mouth of Marten Creek. It was a long day. Was well past dark before I got home but as I got close to the cabin I saw the light in the window, could hear the radio playing, and see smoke and sparks rising from the stovepipe. Made me feel like the long day was worthwhile knowing there'd be hot tea waiting. As I got closer the dogs started barking and Son came out.

"*Hi Dad, did you get anything?*" he called out in an excited voice. Then Mom stuck her head out and said, "*You sure had a long day. Tea's on.*" Daughter's little smiling face looked up at me while she held on to Mom's leg. All I can say is it's a good life! I thank God. Maybe that Christian radio station we listen to is getting to me?

The next day was even longer. I got to where I stopped yesterday; caught a marten – a big nice dark one – at least a $50 bill. I cached it in a tree by the last set I made and went on up Marten Creek. It's a nice day, just barely can see the sun for a little while to the south before it goes behind a mountain. There's only an inch of snow on the ground but it's only ten degrees above zero and things are froze up good but we need more snow so I can use the dogs.

It's very important to blaze trail when going up a brushy ridge or you'll lose your trail and might lose traps. You see, once you make a set on your trapline you just spring traps at the end of season leaving them hanging to be re-baited and set next year. No sense taking traps in cuz on these wild country trap lines you are the only one fool enough to wander around out there anyway. So don't need to worry about theft.

So this line is done, time to head home. It's already dark and I'm hungry. I picked up the marten I cached, went on my way and caught another where the caribou kill was. Tomorrow I'll set line down river to moose kill on beaver pond.

Woke up in the morning about 5:30, got the fire

going, put the coffee pot on, and got back into the bag till it warmed and the coffee started to perk. We've kerosene railroad lamps for light. They do give enough light but no extra. Six gallons of kerosene seem to last us the three months we're out on the trapline. Anyway, get the first cup down sitting in front of the stove. By then it is 6:00 a.m. and the radio station we can get is on. I turn it on and start breakfast and give Mom a cup of coffee. The kids are still asleep. Got caribou steaks a-fryin and hotcakes with blueberry syrup. I'm hungry and I eat aplenty. Kids are still asleep another half hour so I drink coffee and listen to the radio.

It's finally light enough to load up pack with bait and extra traps and with my trail axe in hand head down to the beaver pond. It snowed another inch and is overcast. Maybe we'll get some more snow. There are about eight marten sets I put out along the way to the beaver pond. At the beaver pond around moose kill there's a lot of activity. I put a wolverine set out on the hill and place about eight marten sets around the beaver pond. I think we'll have a few marten shortly.

Now it's only about 11 a.m. so I went home and am thinking about going on past the beaver pond, head up the creek we came down and set out that line and get the toboggan so I can use the dogs. Need to get things ready. I will pack the dogs including their harnesses to pull the toboggan down. With only two or three inches of snow it will be tough coming back. I'll be gone four days settin line out but it will only take three days to check each time.

I have the dog packs already loaded up to put on the dogs. My pack is ready and it's time to kiss the wife "good-bye" and hug the kids. We leave and make good time. Won't have to stop and set traps for the first two and a half miles cuz I did that yesterday. As I start up the creek above the beaver pond I see some sign of marten moving around. I've all the sets made from the previous years, mostly pole sets and some ground sets for wolverine. All I need to do is bait sets and set the traps that are already there. As I said earlier, I use pieces of dry dog salmon for marten bait, but for wolverine I use a piece of lower leg bone of caribou or moose. I wire it tightly and then staple the wire to a tree using fencing staples, hanging it about one and a half feet off the ground. This set is put right next to the trail. The wolverine comes along the trail stealing from marten sets, sees the bait, goes after it, and if he doesn't step in the trap right off, he will while he fights to pull off the bait and you got yourself a piece of fur that's worth probably five marten.

I cover the trap by first chopping out the ground underneath so the trap will be level with the ground around it then lay a few pieces of dry spruce boughs down, setting the trap on top. To cover the trap, I find a big spruce tree with a couple of large roots coming out from it. There is usually a big bed of dry, dead, spruce needles. These I shovel into a gunny sack for covering wolverine sets. I pour out enough to cover the trap, spread them out with spruce bough and take a twig and pull any out that's wedged under the trap-pan that would stop trap from springing. The pan should be no higher or lower than the jaws of the trap.

So, as I go up I set traps and cut out anything that fell in the trail that would be in the way of the toboggan when I bring it down from the upper cabin. Things went according to plan and I got to Moose Lick cabin – an eleven mile day. It wasn't quite dark. After getting the fire going and tea water on, I sawed up some more wood. I'd be using this cabin at least seven times before we'd leave the trapline so will need enough wood to not have to cut it each night. As the winter progresses it gets down to less than six hours of daylight.

It feels about zero temperature outside and is partly cloudy. By the time I drink a cup of tea and saw up some wood it's getting dark out. It's dark inside the cabin so I light a plumber's candle. It burns slow enough to last as long as I need it before I go to sleep and till I leave in the morning. I always cache a dozen in each cabin.

Each cabin is also outfitted with a frying pan, cooking pot, plates, cups and forks and spoons and such. Also, I leave a bedroll in each cabin so I won't have to carry much. After I get the toboggan running I freight enough grub to each cabin so I won't have to haul grub each time either. I even haul some dry fish. This way the less the dogs have to pull, the more you can ride, and the less you'll get tired. My personal feed bag is: fry meat, fry bread, and gravy for supper and for breakfast it's fry meat and boil up a pot of rice, drain it, pour rice in frying pan of meat, stir it up and eat it all. Now, that's putting on the feed bag!

The next day it's only six miles to the upper cabin and I continue up, setting traps on the trail here rather than farther down the creek because of wind so it took some time, but we finish the line. Dogs behaved well. They didn't fight or run off and lose their packs. The cabin's in good shape. Toboggan is okay and it looks like we've got plenty of wood. I brought the dog harnesses along so I get them strung out and ready for tomorrow.

The next day I had a few wolverine traps to set out so went up and got them out on a ridge that goes up above the timberline. I chopped a small tree down and carried it up the ridge and set the last trap above the timberline and wired the trap to the tree I carried up. I shoved the bait into the hole, laid a little brush on the hole, and then covered the trap lightly with moose hair and a little snow to weigh the hair down. It's definitely below zero today cuz the icicles on my mustache are substantial.

It's still early so I get back to the cabin, hook up the dogs, and head out to home. It's a rough ride and a lot of the time I'm running to keep the toboggan from tipping over. There's a marten in a trap before we get to Moose Lick cabin. It doesn't seem too late in the day so we press on. Halfway to the beaver pond there's another marten. It's already dead and half frozen – a large, good-colored male. By the time we're at the beaver pond it's getting toward dark but at the kill there's two more marten – one in a pole set, the other in the wolverine set and he's a little hard to get out of the trap. They curl up, but I got it out, reset the trap and headed home.

The kids and Mom are happy to see me and I them. Mom has an ability to keep busy and take charge while I'm gone and kids are very creative and can invent things to do and also, Son has school work. So they have as much to tell me as I them. We're a pretty good team for this kind of life. Mom also has two apple pies made – one for her and the kids and one for me. I finish the last piece of pie for a midnight snack when I get up to put more wood in the fire.

The next day I hauled wood with the toboggan. At least I don't have to haul it in on my shoulders a log at a time. Hauled the wood from the wood yard we cut this fall. Did this all morning and had a couple of weeks' worth. Then in the afternoon I skin marten and watch daughter while Son and Mom go set out the little trapline. It's a good life. It's snowing outside. They come back all excited with high hopes of catching marten and rabbits (Snowshoe Hares).

There's more snow out now and today I'll set out the last line. It's only five miles long. That will give me thirty miles of line. So after breakfast I start out. I'll run the dogs straight back behind the cabin and across a flat then onto the river going on upriver for a couple of miles. Had a few traps to set on the way then at the mouth of a creek I tied up the dogs and put on my packboard and started up the ridge. It's two miles to the timberline and fairly steep. As I go up setting traps, I blaze the trail a little better. I get to the top and man, it's a pretty view. The trapline is all set out. Now we'll see what we catch this season.

We get into a weekly routine. Mondays I'd go up the long line, stay overnight at Moose Lick, then next day go to upper cabin, chain up the dogs, put on snowshoes and go up the ridge to check the wolverine sets. Wednesdays, I go back home; get there by 2 p.m. The next day check the eight-mile line then stay around the cabin and family, skinning and stretching the fur I caught that week and hauling and cutting wood. I'd be able to run more miles of traps if I could make loops but the country didn't seem to permit that to happen where my trapline was.

The month of November seems to be the best month to catch marten. I probably caught two-thirds of the catch that month and then it slows down as December goes along. Wolverines are very strong for their size. When in a trap, they will tear up the area as well as the trap. I've seen them bend trap-pans and triggers in such a way it was hard for me to straighten them out.

On the second run up the long line in the last trap on the ridge above the timberline I caught a very large, very blond diamond wolverine. Somehow the trap caught him on the hind foot. He was mad and it was quite a dance to hit him on the head with the flat end of the axe. But it got done and I didn't get bit. We caught three wolverines that season. Two were large, the blond and a dark one. I sold them for $275 each and caught a smaller female on moose kill and sold her for $250. I did lose about six marten to wolverine that would have brought me $300 but those three wolverines brought

$800 so they more than compensated for the theft. I also had three marten damaged by mice pulling hair out of the marten. But Mom made a nice marten hat for Son out of the three so they were used anyway.

Another run on the eight-mile line I jumped a grizzly. I was on the ridge up a creek beside some brush and I heard something break on the other side of the brush. I looked and saw a large grizzly moving around. Then it took off at a run on up the ridge the way I was going. There was a lot of daylight showing under his legs meaning he was an old bear that didn't get enough fat put on to go into good hibernation. I was a little nervous to go on but did and saw that he crossed my trail and kept going. That was the only bear I saw during winter in all the years on the trapline. They are mostly fast asleep all winter.

In November we did pretty well. I'd catch about ten marten a week and in December it slowed down till the last week before Christmas we only got four marten. For the two months trapping we ended up with fifty-two marten and three wolverines. This is just an average season but it made a good wage for us. The traps were already paid for years ago. We couldn't charge the food to trapping expense cuz it would probably cost us more if we stayed home instead of trapping. The only real cost we have is chartering a plane for three flights – two for airdrops and the third comes in, lands on the river, and picks up Mom and the kids and the fur. I mush into town with the dogs, closing down the trapline on my way, and bring in any fur I might catch. Anyway, the plane fare is the only real expense we have. That's only around $300.

The fur auction house I send my fur to, Seattle Fur Exchange, takes a 5% commission for selling and cleaning the fur. (I think it's more now.) I end up selling forty-one martens and three wolverines. The martens sold for $2,255 and the wolverines $800 which equals $3,055. Take out the 5% commission of $152.75 and the $300 plane bill that leaves $2,602.25 which was a fair wage back then.

Some particular trap lines in certain years do better. I've heard of one trapper getting over 200 marten in less than 20 miles of trapline, but that's not all that common. The main reason I trapped only till Christmas was I figured anything caught later is hurting your breeding stock for the next season. Whether I'm right I do not know but that's my reasoning.

About the 17th of December it got pretty cold, about 60 below zero, and we were wondering if the plane would come in on the 19th. Well it didn't and I'd sprung the two shorter lines the 17th and 18th so we were waiting for the weather to get warm enough for a plane to fly out here to pick up Mom, kids and the fur. On the radio station there's a program every night at 9:30 and then in the morning at 6:30 called "Trapline Chatter." If someone wants to get a message to someone on the trapline they call the radio station, tell the message, and the station will broadcast it on "Trapline Chatter." Well the pilot sent a message in and said he'd try to get in to us on the 23rd.

The morning of the 23rd it was a light overcast. It warmed up to minus 40, so he might make it in. If he does it will be a marathon mush for me and the dogs into town. About 9:30 a.m. we heard the plane. We had the dogs hitched to the toboggan ready to go, so we threw our daughter in the toboggan and I headed over to the river where I had marked out the airstrip. The plane landed just as we got there. While we waited for Mom and Son (they had to walk) we loaded the plane with the fur and personal things. Mom and Son arrived soon, boarded the plane and the pilot started the engine. Everyone waved and the plane started off. It got off on the first try.

It was just me and the dogs now. The fire in the stove when we got back to the cabin was out so I set the stove out under the overhang, took the things I didn't want to leave in the cabin to the cache, then tied the door open so the grizzlies wouldn't tear it down. With that done it was time to leave and if I wanted to get into town before Christmas morning I'd best put on the "big skedaddle." As we went along I'd spring the traps. It was well into dark before we got to the Moose Lick cabin. I got a fire going, put on snow to melt (after creeks freeze we melt snow for water), then chained up and fed the dogs, ate dinner, and went to bed.

Next day was Christmas Eve day. We've 36 miles to go today. It's still dark when we leave. It stays that way for the first hour. It's cold too. I've two inches of icicles on my beard already. There's a marten in one trap, then another in the next, and that's it for marten this season.

Get up to upper cabin and I give the dogs a break and I take things I don't want torn up out of cabin and put them in the cache. The next four miles is uphill and I'll be on snowshoes till we're a mile over the pass. Five miles then it's downhill till we come to a creek. There we should run onto another trapper's trail. We do, and the trail is broke out but it's been snowed on and drifted in spots. The dogs have a slow go. I'm kicking off and running some. We pass a cabin I sometimes stop at. We've another hour and it will be dark. I'm sweating and it must be ten miles to the first cabin outside of town. Then it's another ten after that so it's going to be all night to get in for Christmas day.

We're two hours out from the first cabin from town. It's been dark awhile. The dogs and I are getting tired but we've done these marathons before and we've been tired before so we knew what we were getting into. We finally came to the cabin ten miles out of town. We pulled in. I left the dogs in harness and threw them each a dry fish then went in and built a fire, put snow on, and put some frozen chunks of lard and frozen chunks of moose in frying pan. Drink tea, and more tea, and still more tea and by then the meat was done. Threw a handful of flour in, stirred, then poured water on it and stirred some more. Then I threw a couple of frozen biscuits in with the meat and gravy to thaw out a little and ate the whole thing.

I made one near fatal mistake. I lay down on the bunk and I fell asleep. I don't know how long I slept but when I awoke it was cold in the cabin. Well I jumped up and got my parka on and threw what I had taken out of the toboggan back in, untangled the dogs, and put on the "big skedaddle." Times a-wasting and Christmas was here. I guessed it to be 1:00 or 2:00 a.m. We hit the trail. The dogs knew where we were. The trail here is good. Somebody must have come out here for something from town. Then we hit the mining road (cat trail) where they use snow machines and the trail was great. So another one and a half hours and we were in town. We live four miles on the other side of town so pressed on pullin in front of our log home, banged on the door, and yelled for Mom to wake up. She came to the door and I had made it! It was 5:00 a.m. Christmas morning. I didn't know the Lord Jesus Christ then but I thanked Him anyway for getting us all in safely.

After tending to the dogs, I went into the cabin and Mom had a pound of link sausage, three eggs, a mountain of hash browns, and toast ready. It had been awhile since I had any white man grub. It tasted mighty good. The kids would be waking soon to open the presents Mom had bought yesterday. It's a good Christmas. And it was a good season to finish our life on the trapline. We made enough to buy $700 worth of groceries, a two-ton truck for $600, an old sawmill (not assembled) for $400, and a horse for slidin logs for $800. I'd already paid the pilot before we went out on the trapline that season. We quit the trapline and began a logging and rough lumber business. So ends an era in this family's life and we begin another.

I would like to take one more moment of your time to

mention something of my spiritual status. At this time I was a Hell-bound renegade doing exactly what I wanted, living for myself – not even paying a mind to laws, cursing God, drinking and such foolishness. Then this last season on the trapline God started dealing with me through the radio station KJNP North Pole, Alaska, "The Gospel Channel of the North" (and most of the time the only one anyone can get). He convinced me that I was going to Hell and also *"No man by his own works is right with God,"* Romans 3:23. He left me in that state for almost two years. Then God sent a man to tell the Gospel to me that would save me from going to Hell and spending eternity there.

The first thing I had to understand was that *"The wages of sin is death. But the gift of God is eternal life through our Lord Jesus Christ,"* Romans 6:23. But what did He do for us that men who trust Him won't go to Hell? This is what had to be explained to me. It was that He took our sins upon Himself and died in our place and that was the right payment for our sins because He was without sin. No other man could do this because *"all men have sinned,"* Romans 3:23. Then God raised Him from the grave proving *"Jesus is God,"* 1 Corinthians 15:3-4, Romans 10:9. So I found that *"salvation is by faith not by works,"* Ephesians 2:8-9.

Life hasn't been easy now that we trust in Christ but we do have peace with God knowing that we are saved from Hell's eternal pain and suffering. We've a purpose now to serve Christ, not Satan and sin. I praise the Lord for saving my soul.

Appendix

<u>Supplies and Trap sets:</u>

The grub list we had for the last trapping season:
1. 200 lbs. Flour
2. 60 lbs. Sugar
3. 50 lbs. Rice
4. 10 lbs. Dried sliced potatoes
5. 25 lbs. pinto beans (less meat means more beans needed)
6. 10 lbs. salt
7. 1 #10 can of dried vegetables for soup
8. 25 lbs. dried apples
9. 10 lbs. prunes
10. 50 lbs. lard or shortening
11. 3 lb. can yeast
12. 5 cans baking powder
13. 25 lbs. Krustez pancake mix
14. 25 lbs. rolled oats
15. 25 lbs. powdered milk
16. Spices: Pepper, cinnamon, seasoned salt, etc.
17. Case toilet paper and one half-case paper towels
18. 10 boxes strike anywhere matches
19. 6 gal. Kerosene and 50 plumber's candles
20. 5 boxes tea, 3 3 lb. cans coffee
21. 2 cans cocoa mix
22. 4 boxes pectin (for blueberry jam)
23. Dental floss for sewing tough stuff
24. 10 glover's needles for sewing leather

25. 1 large bottle Betadine (cleaning and soaking wounds)
26. Penicillin pills
27. 1 tube good topical ointment
28. Tape and bandages
29. Batteries for flashlight and radio
30. Radio booster and antenna wire and radio
31. Nails assorted sizes, staples
32. 3 mill file
33. Swede saw, 3 extra blades
34. Axes and extra handle
35. Hammer, pliers, screwdrivers, crescent wrench, brace and bits
36. 2 rolls mechanic's wire

There are a few other things you might need but this will start you out and with some common sense you can add to list.

What You Should Wear For Winter Travel:
Wool socks, cotton long underwear, heavy wool long underwear, then blue jeans or heavy canvas pants – either will buck wind ok or moose hide pants, wool shirt, a couple wool jackets then canvas or moose hide parka with a good ruff to keep wind off face, a good stocking cap, moccasins or mukluks for colder weather and snowshoeing and shoepacks for warmer days and getting through wet spots. My wife makes winter parkas, pants, and moccasins out of Indian tanned moose hide. I've a pair of moose hide pants, made by

my wife's mother and a friend, that I've worn since 1973 and they're still in good shape. Moose hide clothes are expensive but last forever. She also makes trail mittens. You'll wear gloves to work in but you'll be wearing mittens most of the time – heavy trail type mitts and lighter mitts. Have plenty of mitten liners and extra felt liners and insoles for moccasins. Frostbite can kill you. Always carry matches in a waterproof case with birch bark or a candle to start fires – never be without.

Free Trappers I've Known

When I came to Eagle in 1971 there were three men who lived and trapped mostly down river from Eagle. Two used dogs and one used a snow machine. He was called Pollack Joe. He ran a long trapline and often people in Eagle would see a light slowly coming up the Yukon and know it was Joe carrying a railroad lantern. He must have broken down again and was coming into Eagle to get parts for his snow machine. He'd probably come up from Nation, a fifty mile walk. He'd get parts and walk back down. He was a good trapper and caught a lot of lynx, marten, and wolf. Later he got partnered up with a fella and they went gold mining out of Chicken. There were others mining nearby and they got in a claim dispute and shot Joe and his partner dead. However, Joe's partner had a .410 shotgun handy and shot one of them in the leg. They were caught later and I believe they are in jail even now. Joe was a hard worker and well-liked by most of the Indians in Eagle village.

In 1972 a young couple came to Eagle after break up. They had an old red pickup with a plywood box and a canoe. They floated down the river about ten miles to the mouth of Shade Creek and there built a cabin. They were green as moldy bread but they were persistent and not lazy. Charlie dug in and asked questions about everything, thought things through, and became as good a trapper, hunter, dog musher, and river man as you'd find. He and others of that wave of frontiersmen earned what they got. They didn't take food stamps or any kind of assistance. If they couldn't make it trapping they would work in the summer for a winter's grubstake.

There were a lot of people going out during the gold rush of 1898. Back then there were trails, roadhouses, and trading posts with everything you needed to travel in the north. This generation had no trails, no roadhouses, or trading posts to get exactly what we needed. So we had to reinvent the wheel, so to speak. However, there were old sleds, harnesses, etc. as well as some of the old-timers who lived in the bush that you could talk to about the country and making things a trapper would need.

There was one young man I came to admire (and I recognize that he was a man made of the right leather) by the name of Randy Brown. He came to my Main cabin on the North Fork of the Fortymile. (It's a three to four day walk to the cabin from Eagle.) Along with a friend of mine that everyone called Little John, I came out there later to hunt meat for the winter. Anyway, they teamed up the following year and went down river to Charlie Creek, now known as the Kandik River. They lined a canoe a ways up and built a couple of cabins and trapped and lived in that country for quite a few years, several of which he never took any rice or flour just ate meat. Randy became a good axe-man, tanned hides, made his own snowshoes; even learned later to make birch-bark canoes. He was a humble, friendly guy and in time was well respected by his peers. By 1976 there were about twelve or thirteen, either couples or single men, scattered along the river from Eagle to Charlie River and its tributaries (about 100 river miles, not counting the miles up the side rivers). Most used a Grumman freight canoe with a 10-horse outboard. They got the skills down to run those shallow fast-moving side rivers freighting up what they needed before freeze up. Just about all of them used dogs in the winter pulling toboggans. They generally had big dogs because they hauled a lot of their outfit and wood.

Most years there were good dog salmon runs in September. Most like me used gillnets but some liked the idea of fish wheels. Two men that liked wheels were Dana Ulvi and my nephew Bill Gobel. (He married my wife's oldest sister's oldest daughter. He's only three years younger than me.) I met Bill on the pipeline and invited him to check out Eagle. He was a very practical thinking man and came up with some good ideas. One problem toboggans had was if you run into overflow (running water on top of the ice) you would about stop when back on the snow because the snow would stick to the wood bottom. He'd seen that was a problem and in a catalog found one-quarter inch poly plastic sheets you could buy and bolt on the toboggan bottom. Now you could go into the overflow and back onto the snow and keep on going. He became a good trapper and started a trapline above mine on Slate Creek.

Bill and Dana were a lot alike and they became good friends. They did a lot of traveling by dog team together as well as built and ran fish wheels. Dana was a deep thinker, studied on a project, and always wanted everything as efficient as possible. So when they teamed up on anything it turned out good. They had quite a few dogs between them so they needed a couple thousand salmon for winter. One trip they took with the dogs was the old winter trail that the old Indians used to get into the Ogilvie River country across the border into Yukon Territory. You gotta remember this was years later than when it was used regularly by the Indians of Eagle. The trails were grown over, they had to cut a new road out, and have enough of an outfit to travel with in temperatures that might get minus 40 or colder: feed for them and the dogs, tent, wood stove, axe, saw and so on. That's steep, rocky country. You need to know how to slow going down steep grades. Once you are on Sheep Creek, it's a good size river running through canyon country, you soon run into a pretty tall waterfall. You have to go up, and with a rope and block and tackle, you have to wedge a log into a crack in the ice, tie the block on and pull the toboggans up. Then it widens out into beautiful country. As I remember, they shot a couple of caribou and brought them back.

Ol Bill had guts too. His trapline was 70 miles out from town. There was an old airstrip some miners hacked out on a ridge between Gold Run and Jim Creek. So he'd hire a local pilot to fly him, his family, and his outfit there. It was more than a two mile hike to the cabin he built so there were quite a few packs to get his outfit down to his camp. (He'd airdrop some things but still had much to pack.) As I remember he'd pack his dogs too. Well one of the trips up there they ran into a sow grizzly with cubs. One of his dogs took out after it and soon it was the grizzly that was chasing his dog. Well a couple times the two ran across in front of him about 30 feet out. He got a shot off each time and didn't slow her down one bit. Then the dog turned and came right at Bill. His third shot took the old sow in the head at ten feet. That put her down. It takes some courage to stand your ground in that situation and not let fear have its way with you. You never know till you're faced with that kind of situation just what you'll do. "*Courage is not the absence of fear but the ability to do what's needed in spite of the fear.*" (My definition based on experience).

There were a lot more stories like these men who made their living out there off the land but that's enough to show you what these men and women were made of: "The Right Stuff." I remember they'd get together and talk about what they were going to do and when they were ready they would get it done right. Fact is most of these men were like that. Plan what you are going to do knowing that there isn't a store or anybody nearby to help you out. None of them were fat and they weren't lazy or they wouldn't last.

There was a get-together once that me and my wife and kids went to. My wife took a picture of them and us (about 25 in that picture: men, women and their kids). A fellow that was in the thick of it in the Viet Nam war saw that picture. *"Looks like a fine bunch of guerrilla fighters,"* he said. They were.

"Free Trappers" was what they were called. They could move through that far away North Country like they were part of it – and they were. My hat's off to them. I don't think there will be too many more like them. May the Lord have mercy on their souls and give them faith in Jesus as their Lord and Savior.

Vision of a Sodbuster

The last year on our trapline was in the mountains, forty-eight miles southwest of Eagle, Alaska, which is where the Yukon River comes through the border from the Yukon Territory. We had a good season in 1979; I trapped from October to Christmas. I had a good catch of marten and a few wolverines.

My son was on correspondence schooling, as I took my wife and two kids out there with me. It was a good life, but I could see we weren't doing a good job teaching our eight-year-old son. He needed to be in school.

After Christmas I'd cut cordwood for sale. I'd cut and stack it, then hire a fella who had a CAT and a good size bobsled to haul it. I'd give him one load and then I'd sell two loads. It got me thinking back on my earlier years here in Alaska working as a horse guide packing hunters and geologists in the mountains. We had a team we'd use for various work and I wondered if it would pay to get a horse or two and use them for loggin. The old road to Eagle was snowed in till mid-April back then. So when it opened up I thought I might go out on the road and see if I could find a horse.

But before that I'd go see about an old "Bell Saw"

sawmill out the road 35 miles or so. So I hooked up my dog team and had a look. They wanted $400 for it. As much I could see, it was all there so I bought it. (I had no idea how to set it up let alone run it.) Now I knew I'd need a truck to haul the logs. There was an old mechanic in town that had an old Ford two-ton '64. He wanted $600 for it. It ran good, which was important cuz back then I wasn't much of a mechanic. Truth was I didn't know a thing. My wife was an Indian from there and my life in Alaska up to then was learning and then becoming a pretty fair mountain man who lived by the gun and the trap. Well God was turning a new chapter in my life. Like most visions in my life it expanded larger than I first thought and in a couple years I'd be starting a farm. We'll get to that a little later.

Ya know back in my mountain man days I thought it was me alone making things the way I wanted and that sometimes I was lucky and sometimes down on my luck. But here in this new chapter of my life I was beginning to understand I was really being directed by something greater than me.

Anyway middle of April came and a good part of the winter's snow was melting away. I got a friend of mine to help me with his pickup. My two-ton truck needed some lumber for the flatbed before I could use it. Hence I needed to get the sawmill so I could set it up and cut some boards. While I was doing cordwood I was thinking ahead a little and had a load or two of saw logs stacked up. Well I had no idea how to set that mill up but as I was about to start a fella from Colorado, who grew up horse logging and running a portable sawmill, came drifting into Eagle. After the road opens in the spring we always got a few "characters" of an interesting nature that come rolling in looking things over. Some would stay but most moved on. This one moved on, but traded a meal of caribou steaks for laying out the sawmill and explained how to cut boards. I don't think I could have set it up without him showing me, and me writing down and making a diagram of the mill.

I had an old International pickup that didn't run too good, so I talked to the local mechanic to see if he could help me out. He got it running pretty fair without too much from my pocket. So now I had power to run the mill. I jacked up the backend, blocked the front tires, and by attaching the flat-belt from the right tire to the mill mandrel-pulley the moving parts moved the direction they were supposed to, at least after the second or third adjustments.

Well I'll not forget the first log I sawed. I was a bit scared, but the blade was turning right. When I pushed the lever forward the carriage moved down the track. So I put the log on the head blocks and drove log dogs in the log and the first slab was cut off. Pulled back on the lever and the log came back, turned the log cut side down and cut off the next slab. Two more turns, and I was cutting lumber. The mill had a ratcheting lever that pushed the log out, but didn't have a measure, so I didn't know where one inch or two inches was. Plus you had to allow for the width of the saw blade, so I had to "Joe McGee" a meter which worked okay.

That first summer I just milled out enough to build an addition to our house and sold a little. Believe me, I had many trials and tribulations that might have caused me to quit before I got it going. Now I needed a horse to skid logs. It wasn't until the end of May, after I set up and got the mill running and put a deck on that ol two-ton truck that I set out horse hunting. There's an agriculture area toward Fairbanks called The Delta Barley Project. I found an old guy from eastern Colorado who brushed out hay and barley farms, but also ran 30 to 40 head of Hereford cows and I saw in his corral a horse. Turned out his son brought him home from a bucking string and had no use for him. The horse had a big head with wild eyes, short legs and a thick body. They said he was part Clyde and part Broomtail. Well, I didn't know where else to look for a horse so I bought him and some hay, and from the Delta Co-op I bought some C.O.B.

I heard of a fella down toward Birch Lake that had some experience working horses. Went there and got a collar that would fit Pappy which was the horse's name. I already had a harness. It was given to me by an ol guy who used to cut wood for the steamboats back before WWII. He'd had a horse to skid wood out upriver from Eagle (Yukon River). I asked Joe Meek, the guy I bought the collar from, for advice on how to break a horse to pull. That wasn't too good advice I found out later after I don't know how many "runaways." By the way that was the summer of 1980.

Now I grew up having saddle horses in Iowa and

when I was first up in Alaska I learned the packing trade and how to shoe horses while I worked some horses skiddin logs. I'd never tried breaking one to pull, much less a wild-eyed bronc. I remember one runaway in particular. I was skidding sixteen-foot house logs from a raft of logs tied up on the river beach. I skidded them up the beach to top of the bank. Those days if you wanted house logs, you'd go upriver, cut them down, pull um out to the river, make a raft, and float them down to the village where my wife's people the Han Indians are. (People of the River) Anyway I was skidding them up and boy, Pappy was a handful trying to run them up. One time he got away from me and instead of running away from the river, turned and jumped in. Ya know it's an interesting sight to see a horse in harness swimming down the river pulling a log. He finally came ashore. Right where Matthew Malcom had set out a white fishnet! The log hit the end of the fishnet and went up the length of it peeling the mesh off the cork line. It ruined that net. Now I had just bought a new white fishnet and of course, I gave him mine and took his, and repaired it for my own use.

Back in those days there was no electricity. We used the fishnets to catch fish to feed our families and dog team. In the spring and summer it was either, dried meat, soup, and pinto beans or fresh fish. We shot caribou and/or moose in the fall and winter then dried some for spring and summer. Well that summer, Pappy didn't get much better. In the fall we used him packing out some moose and caribou and rode him some and he did good. But skidding logs he was a little spooked.

The ol guy who gave me the harness told me how he broke his horse. He learned from an old Wyoming cowboy who came to Alaska and became one of the first game wardens in the interior. What he told me made sense and I used it on Pappy and every horse thereafter that I broke to pull. What you do is tie him behind a truck and hook him to a log just big enough so he knows he's pulling something. Then you drive along slow. The horse will try to stop and then lunge forward and do that for a while till he finally gets bored with the whole thing and plods along. It depends on the horse; some learn quick and some take a few days. Anyway more about breaking horses later on. That did the trick. I could drive Pappy now without expecting a runaway.

I found a pretty good bobsled in the brush by an old cabin. I had to replace some of the wood that made up the bunks. I hired somebody to weld 3/8" steel plates on two 2" pipes. The plates were 3/8" x 3" x 8." They had about 4" sticking out past the end of the pipes. A mechanic torched out a 1" hole in the center of the plates. Then I took the nuts off the front bob spreader and put on the pipes with plates, one on each side. I put the nuts back on and I had shafts. Then I put Pappy's harness's back-pad on each side with solid copper rivets. I put on straps with buckles for the shafts. Then with a light chain I fastened the singletree.

It was now October. Freeze up and snow were here, time to think about cordwood. I found I could load 12' lengths on the bobsled and bring in an honest cord in three trips. Later with a team, I'd bring in a cord at a time. But it was working. I got a sawmill for $400, a truck for $600, a horse for $800, so by the time I got everything working I imagine I spent $2,400. I had made $3,000 that last year on trapline. I was able to get some groceries bought (flour, rice, etc.) so my family didn't starve. Also that summer I called B.L.M. in Tok, Alaska and asked about me buying timber for the Sawmill. On the Yukon River there were some islands with timber on them – white spruce gets big enough for saw logs. I was able to have some trees marked on an island across the river from the boat landing at Eagle.

I need to explain a few things. I was more fortunate than many. While I've always made a living for me and my family, I had some mighty fine parents. Dad had a good business in Iowa. My sister and I grew up on twenty acres. Our mom ran a ten-acre apple orchard and we had some horses to ride. But the city was creeping out into the country like a lot of cities do. By the late 70s there were developers eyeing my folk's twenty acres as well as those surrounding us. Dad knew another twenty for sale and loaned me and my sister the money. We bought it, then turned around and sold it, paid Dad back and the IRS, and had $15,000 or so apiece for me and my sister. So I had a little to start out with.

The timber back then was cheap: $32 per 1,000 board feet. That little sale had only about 10,000 or 12,000 board feet. So the cost was only about $360. Later I found selling the slabs for firewood paid for the timber.

I was almost ready to start, only had to wait for the ice to get frozen good. Now the Yukon River by February will get five feet of ice in most places. The way I planned to log that island was to drive the truck across the river, back the truck to a cut bank, put a couple log rollers on the truck and roll the logs on crosswise. I had cut skid roads the length of the sale down the middle back in the fall before freeze up. I went over by boat with my chainsaw that way there wouldn't be so many stumps in the way of the logs I was skidding.

Up in that country, December and January are pretty short on daylight. On the shortest day (if ya had a good imagination) you could maybe ring out from can't see to can't see. Maybe six hours of kinda can see on both ends of can see, and there can be a fair bit of minus 40 to minus 60 degrees Fahrenheit. So we started the logging in February. Now later I learned it takes less timber to make a living if you fall, limb, buck, skid, and load yourself. But starting out I hired a hand to run the saw and help load.

Now the fella I had in mind, at first I didn't like him hanging around. He was one of them sissy born-again Christians. I was a foul-mouthed renegade back in those days and he made me feel uncomfortable. (Truth is he made me recognize my sin.) For some reason though I wouldn't run him off. Later I liked the peace he had about him and we became friends. So I hired him. Told him I couldn't pay him till I sold some lumber next summer and he agreed.

So we started. There was too much snow to get to the

island, but the postmaster had a 350 John Deere CAT he was willing to use to clear out a road for me. I had chains on so that helped, but I needed a road. Ya see when those big northern rivers freeze, what happens is the ice forms in little islands and the colder it gets, the more there are and they get thicker, and the ice on the beach reaches further out and pretty soon they jam up. Well then, the thinner edges get shoved up vertically as the ice jams to a stop, so there really isn't any flat surface of river ice. And so whether crossing the river with the dog team or a snow machine it's a little slow picking your way across the path of least resistance. In this case we had to use a CAT to push a road across so we could start.

The routine was I'd get up in the morning and light the propane weed burner. I had wired up about six foot of stovepipe; one end was against the oil pan of the truck engine and the other end on the ground where I'd put the torch. The flame wouldn't reach the engine, only heat. It would take 20 to 40 minutes till you could start up the truck, but you wouldn't have to cold start it. I'd take a thermos of hot tea and sandwiches along the four mile drive to the city of Eagle. The city of Eagle is where the white folks lived back in 1981 maybe 60 strong, while the Village of Eagle was three miles upriver where the Han Indians lived about 30 strong. We lived about a mile past. I'd drive down and pick up Steve Hamilton, the Christian fella, and my horse.

The old man that used to cut wood for the steamboat had a little one-horse stable that I'd keep my horse in.

We'd harness him up and tie him to the back of the truck and drive slow to where we crossed the river, then on over to the island where my timber sale was. I'd untie the horse and back up to the island. Steve would go on ahead and start dropping trees, limb, and buck them into the length I'd want. Then shortly I'd follow out with Pappy and start skidding to the deck. I've tried different ways to hook up the logs to the singletree or later doubletree, log tongs and log dogs, but still the best I think is an eight-foot log chain with slide hooks on either end. That way if need be, you can skid out more than one log at the singletree or doubletree, attach a grab hook and swivel (logs tend to rollover some). You can just hook a link at the end of the log but you want horse or horses close to the log. Also if the log you're starting to skid gets stopped by a stump, log or rock, turn the hook so it's the opposite of the direction your horse is going with the chain coming back over the top of the log. When the horse or horses start pulling the log will spin and usually pop over what it's stuck on. Necessity is the mother of invention. At the deck you need to have a cant hook and a good pry bar to move the logs so you can roll and move them when you need to. Organizing your deck for horse logging is important along with the lay of the land in combination with what and how you're going to load, whether it's a truck, wagon, or a bobsled.

One trick I learned is when you need to stack the logs, cuz you don't have much room, put the log deck next to a good, tall, stout tree and hope you're half monkey.

Shinny up that tree with a string tied to your butt, the other end to a long log chain maybe twelve-foot up. Hook that chain around the tree, then it's okay to fall down and break your leg (only joking). Hook the other end to a log tongs when you skid up to the deck. Hook the log tongs somewhere about the middle of the log. Start the horses pulling again and the log will come off the ground. You turn the horses at the head of the deck to the side. The tree is then able to stop um, and let the log settle on to the stack. You can stack three to four high this way. I learned this from an old horse logger later on when I was logging in Wyoming and log trucks with a log loader was hauling logs for us. The forest service sometimes didn't give you much room for a deck.

Let's get back to February 1981. Now I'd skid logs to the deck and some would be 20 feet 8 inches. Logs that my hand cutter would mark to cut at 8 foot or 10 foot to buck in two pieces at the log deck. In Alaska back then with that first sawmill I had, 12 foot was the longest log I could cut. About 3:00 p.m. in the afternoon we'd start rolling logs on to the truck crosswise. Now logs taper, so the butts roll faster than the small ends. You got to cock them so they end up on the truck instead of the beach. There were a lot of small logs in that sale and that was our first year logging any kind of production. Later on by myself I could finish the sale in seven to ten days with a team instead of a single horse, but this sale took about twenty days. Ya have to start somewhere learning, and that island was a good place to start.

Pappy was always a little quick on the pull, but that was my fault starting him wrong. However he was an honest horse. He'd get down low to the deck and pull a heavy log and he was a fair saddlehorse too and could pack a load of meat.

We got finished with the sale toward the end of March. I started up the mill after the snow was pretty much gone, only to find out solid tooth blades are hard to maintain. For about a month I fought those monsters. The problem is after you sharpen them so many times the tooth becomes short, then you'd have to "gum" the blade out and swage the tooth which means to make it wider than the blade. Finally after not being able to cut anymore I found an outfit that makes insert-tooth blades. That was the ticket. I had to sell my freight canoe to do it. The outfit cost me $550, but it finally came. I slapped her in and started up the ol pickup. She was turning good, so I pulled up on the throttle. It started wobbling till it got to the right rpms. Then she stood up straight, sounded good, ran the first log through, she cut it like butter and I was in business.

My son was about ten-years-old then. He worked with me most of the slabs and lumber. He could pack and stack. We worked pretty good together. I'd pay him for any work I'd make money on. Work for our home and family I'd expect him to work without pay. I'd pay him by the day and grade him A, B, C, D, and E. A was $5, B was $3.75, C was $2.50, D was $1.25, and E was when he really messed up or got lazy. Then he'd pay me $5. He didn't get but a couple "E" days. This way he learned to be a good worker. He got to be a good horseman as well as dog musher.

Eagle is pretty isolated so my lumber went fast. Before the end of July it was all sold. But it wasn't the best lumber and that old mill, I had my hands full to keep it cutting. I heard of a portable sawmill called "Mobil Dimension" and later saw one. So I called the company and raised enough money to buy one. It turned out to be just what I needed. It cut very accurate lumber, was portable, I could take it apart, move it and set it up the same day, and it all fit in my bobsled or a pickup.

Just before the road to Eagle closed for the winter, the portable sawmill was ready and landed in Fairbanks from Portland, Oregon. Brought it back in an October snowstorm, but we made it. Eagle is on the Yukon River at the end of a narrow gravel mountain road that took some getting used to. (Later in the tail-end of the last century they paved it from the start up to about 60 to 70 miles.) In Eagle City, I'd bought two lots 50 x 100 feet and set up the sawmill. The land had a good view of the river.

There was a superintendent of the school district that Eagle was in who was an interesting character. He was the son of a horse trader from Witten, South Dakota. He liked to hunt, flew a Super Cub, and liked to "horse trade." Well as time went on, I didn't use the old sawmill. He wanted those two lots and I wanted a lot to build a house to rent and later sell. He bought a lot from someone and traded that lot with some boot money for my two lots and swapped the sawmill for some horse-drawn equipment. I was starting to think about some more horses and clearing some land for hay and potatoes.

I have a hard time in my mind to put in order the events that happen and the year I did the different work of developing the farm and sawmill business. I'll try to get it right as well as recognize the Lord's hand in all this. It was back on that first timber sale that the Christian fella Steve was working. Even before, when we were on the trapline all we could get on the radio was KJNP the gospel channel of the north. I caught on that I was definitely a sinner bound for Hell. Well, God lined up Steve to work for me. When the day came for me to ask the most important question I ever asked, *"How do I get out of going to hell when I die,"* he explained that I couldn't do anything; that Christ Jesus already did what was needed. That is, Jesus paid God's requirements for man's debts (sin). Jesus died on the cross, was buried, took our sins to hell and three days later arose alive. He promised we who believe in what Jesus did, yet though we die we shall live forever with Him. So God granted me repentance to salvation and started my life "anew." This began a change in my worldview though not without growing pains. It took time (years) to do less of my will in His name and more of just His will. This is the growing process that will continue till He brings us home; for our citizenship is now in heaven, we are just pilgrims passing through this world.

Anyway I believe for the next two years I used a single horse for skidding logs. I'd take the sawmill apart and haul it to the timber sale, set up the mill, and skid the logs to the mill in the woods. Then later, the fella with the CAT and bobsled would come and haul out a load of lumber about 2,500 board feet at a time. This would have been the winter of 1981 – 1982.

It was across American Creek, West Eagle City; I was living four miles from town and our timber was two miles past town. The first day I'd ride my horse the six miles to work and we'd fall, limb, buck, and skid till we had 1,000 board feet in front of the sawmill deck. We had a wall tent out there with a Yukon stove, we could build a fire and warm up and eat our lunch. Then the next day I'd take my dog team with five gallons of gas for the mill and cut till the deck of logs were sawed up. Now in November and February I'd set a tripod up near the head of the mill and hang a gaslight. I started it up about 3:30 or 4:00 p.m. so we could finish up in the dark, then head home. Steve would walk the two miles from his house to work on days I skidded. He'd walk back on days I ran the dog team or when not uphill he'd ride. I'd usually get home about 7:00 p.m. only to leave next morning about 7:00 a.m. But we were making a livin.

I'd have to make up some winter shoes for old Pappy. We'd weld re-bar across head and toe and grind them sharp. Later I learned about buying the shoes from the Amish in Iowa with drill tek on them and to use hoof pads so the snow would not ball up on their feet.

Anyway logging like this we could get at least 10,000 board feet a month (20 days a month cutting) November, February, and March – 30,000. In summer of 1982, there were some guys that had me custom log and mill out some logs for them (about 20,000 board feet). I was making a living, Praise the Lord. That summer when we were custom logging and milling, Sonny would ride Pappy skidding logs. I'd be at the mill and the fella who had the trees to be milled would be in the woods. That worked good. I think Sonny that summer was the richest kid in Eagle.

Also that summer I asked the school board if they'd let me try to clear an acre or so on the school-grounds and try planting oats for hay. I had to drive out to Delta Junction, Alaska to buy hay and haul it back. I didn't like that. That ol mountain road wasn't a lot of fun hauling a load of hay over. I was going to have to do it for the next three years till I'd get enough hay land cleared. Anyway, the school board said yes, so I did. Later I found out it belonged not to the school, but part of the state land that circled around Eagle City. However, I never had any trouble. Our house was on my father-in-law's native land allotment. My wife and I had permission to clear some land on his allotment and with what was on the state land we had about 14 acres in hay and potatoes. But that was later. For now I'd clear two acres on what I thought belonged to the school.

I didn't have any farm equipment yet, so just by hand I broadcasted Cayuse oats and some fertilizer. The ground was terrible wet after the permafrost started to thaw and to make matters worse, I had John Borg push the berm piles with his CAT the wrong direction across the slope. They should have been with the slope and since they weren't they made dams as the ground thawed out. (Live and learn.) Carving the farm out of the Alaskan bush, not knowing anything, had its humbling moments as you'll see.

The CAT track scratched the ground up and that helped the seed. It came up, but a lot of the ground was a pretty good duck pond. I learned that Cayuse Oats are short, not good for hay, but cut what there was using a hand scythe like how the old-timers I'd heard about put up a lot of wild hay. Those old-timers would maybe have a single horse and put up hay with a scythe. Now the eastern interior is dryer than the coast, but it seemed like it wasn't many days apart till it rained a little. So they put up "hay cocks." That's a pole drove in the ground and sticking up about four or five feet. About eight inches above the ground you nail on cross pieces. This way you can put the hay on green. It'll dry on the cocks. It's cone-shaped so it sheds water pretty well. That first time cutting hay with a scythe was interesting. You learn to cut it and pull it a little and you'll make a windrow. It takes a while to catch on, but it works.

Also that summer of 1982 I'd bought an old 1962 Ford half-ton pickup – cheap. It didn't have a back axle, but I knew another wreck that did. So got it running, loaded my wife and kids up and drove to White Horse, Yukon Territory, Canada, to scout out horses and hay.

I'd heard there was somebody not far east of Dawson that was cutting and selling hay. I stopped in on the way to White Horse to talk to him about bringing a load of hay to Eagle to sell. There were a few of the white folks that had some milk goats.

I had one now too as well as Pappy. He had a team of horses he used for hauling loose hay for his own use but had a tractor and equipment for haying and bailing.

This area was the old, wild, hay meadows of the old Klondike Gold Rush by Dawson. They'd drained it and cleaned up the brushy areas, but later somebody planted timothy and broam grass. We stayed the night, nice family; this fella was a cowboy type from eastern Colorado. His first homestead was north a little from Wasilla, Alaska, back in the 50s. Then in 1979 or 1980 he moved to the Dawson area cuz Wasilla was getting civilized. I can't remember his name. Anyway, my kids had a good time playing with his. My daughter Jody was five now and Sonny (Patrick) was 11-years-old.

We traveled on up toward White Horse, camping along the Yukon River above the mouth of the White River. The White is a glacier-fed river, milky gray in color. The Yukon is clear blue, beautiful and from Carnaks on South Lodge Pole Pine there starts nice looking mountain country. A lot of hunting guides in that neck of the woods use horses. They turned them loose in the winter; lot of Montana Bunch Grass and Pea vine. However I didn't find any teams. West of White Horse I found a family who was farming and had a feed store. Agriculture was starting and also people were getting affluent enough to have "hobby" horses as they were paving the roads. A lot of the guides weren't letting their horses loose anymore. So there was a demand for hay. He also had a big Percheron stud and he bred them to some Canadian Broomtail mares. He had one mare with foal. Little did I know, but a couple years later I was going to buy this stud colt and breed him to a mare I had and she would throw a fine horse colt.

I bought a little feed for Pappy, the goat, and the chickens then we headed home. That fall I was able to buy some timber from the Indian Land Corporation which was nice. I found a good stand of timber just about four miles southeast of our house and the village.

I borrowed John Borg's big bobsled and rented a 450 John Deere CAT from the Indians to haul lumber and slabs back to our yard to stack. The rent was cheap so it worked out. I first had to cut a "CAT road" through the bush then after it snowed I loaded the mill, tent, stove and a 55 gallon drum of gas for the mill and hauled it out to where I cleared a site for setting up a sawmill.

One thing trapping in the bush teaches you is to solve logistical problems first, second to organize, and third to improvise. As I look back, those of us that set out in the bush and carved out a trapline were in the "school of hard knocks" and either graduated with a degree as logistical engineers or dropped out. I know this school had prepared me for many challenges later on as I'm sure it did for others of that country and times too. It would be good to read a book called "*A Land Gone*

Lonesome" by Dan O'Neill. Two characters in the book who are a good example of what I'm explaining are Randy Brown and Dave Evans.

So solving these problems of setting mill, Cat Road, skid trails and so on, I now could handle. But I sure wanted to get away from using that CAT. I needed a team. I had a subscription to *Draft Horse Journal* that had ads of horse traders across the United States and Canada. Then the Alaska Permanent Dividend Fund started up. Because of the oil revenue, Alaskans paid no state tax of any kind. Now all Alaskan residents would get a dividend check too. It has varied over the years depending on the price per barrel and how the stock market is doing. Because this program is a portion of Alaska Oil, money invested in stocks is directly paid to the residents of Alaska. Sometimes a 1,000 and even up to over 2,000 or so families like us would receive $4,000 to over $8,000. We decided to buy one-way tickets to Seattle, then buy a truck with a stock rack and travel to Iowa where my folks were. Along the way we'd pick up that farm machinery in Witten, South Dakota. In Iowa we'd find a team, load um up, and head back to Alaska. One hitch – it'd be cold cuz January is cold.

We got the truck, it was another 1963, one and a half ton Ford, but it could handle a sixteen-foot bed. Had a mechanic friend in Seattle who I bought the truck from. He had a welder and tools, so had a project to take off the box it had on, extend the frame and move the axles back then put on a 16' flatbed. The truck had two transmissions. The regular 4-speed as well as a browning 3-speed with low, direct, and overdrive gears. After I learned it, that second transmission sure made a difference in driving the Alaska Highway. Back then there was still a lot left unpaved, crooked, and lots of ups and downs. Plus in January the road is snow-packed.

So I headed across from Seattle to Idaho to Montana to Witten, South Dakota. My mechanic friend took me for a ride. The truck ended up in Iowa. I had to put another engine in and later change some other things. But later he made it right with me. Witten was where another friend of mine's father, the Horse Trader, lived. He had the farm equipment and also some well oil and several sets of old, used harnesses. There at Witten, I picked up a plow, a single horse cultivator, a Mitchell Potato Shaker (digger), a dump rake, and a lister which is a plow with a double moldboard. That fall, a friend of a friend of mine came to Alaska to hunt and brought a Sulky Disc, a McCormick #9 mower that he had taken apart and put in his pick up so I could have it in Eagle.

Oh, I'd found a Spike Tooth Harrow in Eagle – two four-foot sections in good shape. Now the truth is, I didn't know a thing about farmin but again I had this vision of what I wanted and like always, I couldn't rest till I got it completed. Looking back it was in accordance with the Lord, cuz he led me through many doors that had to be opened and had me meet the right people at the right time for advice and so on.

Well, I had a flatbed on the truck, but not a stock

rack. My friend's dad had one, so I bought that too. Now that mechanic from Seattle was traveling east with his wife in his pickup and he took my wife and kids on to Iowa to my folks place, cuz I was going to stay with this old horse trader, get equipment, and the stock rack put on. The horse trader thought he might find a team for me too. We looked around his country but we couldn't find anything worth buying. Oh, I forgot to say I also got hooked up with a fella in Rapid City that wanted to pack in the mountains west of Eagle to go hunt. More on that later, but we stopped in Rapid City and he gave me some money.

I had to take that stock rack apart, get it off the horse trader's old truck bed and load it on my truck bed so I could take it to a John Deere Service Shop that I saw on the way. I figured they'd have what I needed to put it on my truck bed the right way so's I could haul horses and equipment all the way back to Alaska. But first I had to get that stock rack apart and loaded on my truck and the horse trader said he'd help, but after the midday meal he took a nap (he was 70, I think) and I started on my own.

The first challenge was the nuts and bolts were rusted tight so with WD40, cheater bars, and box wrenches and maybe an hour later they were all loose. As I remember, I used a hydraulic jack, a Handyman Jack, and a bar lift on them sides, front, and end off that old truck bed. I used brute strength and leverage to load it. About the time I was strapping it down the horse trader came out and was surprised the work was done. He wasn't sure how I did it alone. I was glad he slept. He probably would have told me how to do it and at his age might a got hurt. Well, the Lord blessed me with a strong back and legs, although my arms aren't particularly strong.

The shop finished up the rack on my truck in a couple days. I loaded up the farm equipment and harnesses and headed to Iowa. My family was waiting at my folk's place. Like I said I had a *Draft Horse Journal* and I got busy calling the different ads in the Iowa area to seek out my team. We put on some miles looking and finally found a team of Bay Belgium/Percheron Cross from a horse trader a little west of Iowa City. I think he saw me coming. After I'd bought them one of the horse's mane all of a sudden went over the other side of its neck revealing an abscess that got bad enough that the horse's head was down all the time. So I took him to the Iowa State Vet College and they drove a hypodermic needle in the lump and a stream of puss shot out so far and so fast I never saw where it went. They shaved the hair off, cut into it, and after that they got out the puss. There was a fist-size hole inside. They showed me how to care for it with a betadine solution, warm saltwater mix, and by irrigating it twice a day and penicillin shots, it healed up fairly fast. The area around my folk's place was fast becoming a suburb of west De Moines, but a little west of dad's was a neighbor that had five acres fenced in with a winter antifreeze water tank. He was nice enough to let me put the horses there.

Meanwhile I found out my engine was shot and had

to put another one in, so went to a Ford shop and had them put in another 390 rebuilt engine in the truck. I was spending money twice on this trip it seemed like but was in school you might say. Sometimes starting things are a little tough. I tried hooking the team up to the dump rake and they proved to be a slow but steady team. By now it was the end of January, maybe the 24th or the 26th. The engine and truck seemed ready for our 3,000 mile trip back to Alaska. So we loaded everything up. Because of the cold I had to cover the whole stock rack with a tarp and still have head room for the horses. We solved this problem by putting a 2x4 vertically about one-third of the way back from the front of the rack, wired it to both sides of the rack, nailed a 2x4 and another 4 ft. up and nailed a piece of plywood across to separate the horses from the equipment and our belongings. It was hinged like a trap door so I could get into it to get what we needed as we traveled. I also had a couple of 2x4s lying between the top front of the rack and the 2x4 ridgepole which was between the two vertical 2x4s. Then I laid a sheet of plywood on them. This way I had a pretty good frame to cover with the tarp. When we traveled down the highway the tarp that was tied down well front to back, wouldn't bow inward or flap around. Also ran plywood along the sides so wind couldn't get in. It actually proved to be warm inside. The two big horses let off so much heat. We traveled through some minus 60 degree straight temperatures around Watson Lake on the Alaskan Highway.

We started back for Alaska one morn. I said earlier it was January 24th or 26th but honestly I can't remember. It may have been a little later. This I do remember, it was a long old way back to home. We made good time across. The prairie country highways were good, but we had trouble at the border. The vet that made the health papers out gave me interstate papers and not international papers. Canadian customs sent us back to the American side. I was trying to find a place out of the way to park and find a vet to get this straightened out, when a custom agent came running on waving his arms to stop. So I did and the next thing I know he took my driver's license and had me sit in a chair. Then to his boss he started talking loud enough so I could hear and kept saying, "*He and his truck fits the description.*" I started wondering, what on earth was he thinking?

Finally he let me take the papers to the United States Vet office, in the same building. It took about three or four hours, maybe longer. The custom officers were getting a little tougher all the time. Eventually the older one said, "*By the power vested in me I am going to search your truck.*" So I said, "*Okay let's get at it.*" I tried not to show it, and was forgetting God's in control, but was getting a little angry inside. Then he said, "*Take these horses out!*" I told him I need to find a ramp to back up to. I had a couple planks nailed together so I could carry things in easier that I could slide in between the frame. The customs officer demanded that I use them for the horses and not move my truck. The parking lot was icy. The first horse got halfway down the ramp when the ramp went out from under him. He must have sensed it. He jumped the other way and landed on his feet, but went to his knees, almost falling into a little car nearby. So that was enough for the custom agent. He said the other horse could stay in the truck and he climbed up in. I lifted the trap door for him so he could get in to start taking things apart.

Well, I guess I was helpful and he saw my son was having fun with the ramp, running down and climbing up and he must have decided I wasn't a dangerous drug smuggler after all and said, *"Okay, you can go now."* But I had to wait for my international horse papers. They soon came through and I was directed to a ramp in a railroad yard. My wife sat on the tailgate and led the horse over to that ramp. We loaded up and this time had no troubles with Canadian customs. It was afternoon by that time. I can't recall for sure but I think we made it to Saskatoon before midnight.

The four of us sat in the cab of that ol truck. Adeline put a rolled up sleeping bag between the door and the seat so she is sitting one cheek on the seat and one cheek on the sleeping bag. As I remember, we had some tire trouble the next day, but made it to Dawson Creek, B.C. Bought some hay there and got a room in a hotel. From here on we'd have to be sure there was plug-ins for the trucks where we'd stop for the night so we could plug in our engine heater. This was also the start of the Alaskan Highway. It would be long and slow days with a lot of downshifting of gears up steep hills. I'd shift down to have enough power to get up only to have to stay in low gears to go down those snow-packed downhill grades. Ft. Nelson, Watson L.K., Whitehorse, then Tok, Alaska, they're all about 350 to 450 miles apart, most roads wasn't paved. Going through Waston L.K., it was 62 degrees below. And it was 40 degrees below by the time I got to Tok, Alaska. It took four days to drive the 1,200 or so miles of road, but we weren't the only ones driving up with loaded old trucks. We'd see several and it seemed we'd all end up at about the same places for the night within an hour or two of one another.

Now the horses stayed in the truck from Dawson Creek to the farm I talked about earlier that summer. We went to White Horse. There we unloaded the team no worse for wear. They'd stay there till the road to Eagle opened up in April. We drove the truck to Tok where we flew back to Eagle on the small mail plane. By the time we got back to Eagle it was the first half of February and time to get to logging.

I can't remember while we were gone who looked after our horse. We had a barn by that time for one horse and a goat. I didn't have any place warm enough for the chickens yet, so they became soup. I might have had them watched by the old woodcutter again down in Eagle. I just can't remember. One thing I do remember before we left for the States I had wired the house and barn for electricity cuz the village was starting up a power service. When we got back we didn't light a kerosene lamp, we turned a light switch on. That would have been the February of 1982.

We continued logging and sawing boards till about the first of April. Shortly thereafter the road was plowed open and I went out with a friend in my pickup to Tok. Got the stock truck and drove down toward White Horse to get the team. I tell ya, that's a long ol rough road. It was sure a relief when I pulled into our barnyard with that team. Now I could start figuring the land to clear for our fields.

The Indian village as I said earlier had a John Deere 450 CAT that I could use for a small fee to clear the land. Again I was learning as I went. Some ground was going to take a lot of work draining, while some wouldn't take so long. The land with mostly willows was wetter and later the willows would be determined year after year to come back. I'd learned already which way not to push the berm piles; this time I did that right. I finally got what I paced off. I had cleared the three other fields connected to this land the year before and figured about six or six and a half acres in total. Finally I figured the ground thawed enough to disk. I could use the team again. I was learning as I go. I figured for hay land I would have to plow, but some land was too rough and had too many roots. About half my new land I could see I'd have to plow, pull roots, disk again, and level as good as I could.

I don't remember when or how I heard of *"Small Farmers Journal"* but I found it helpful more so than *"Draft Horse Journal."* But I did get a book called *"Draft Horse Primer"* and it showed how to prepare land and most importantly, how to start out plowing. It said after you make the first furrow, to just drive your team around that furrow with the right horse walking in it, till he was used to it and stays there. Well, old Bay (what I called the right horse of the team and the other Dollar) stayed in there just fine. Probably was the furrow horse on an Amish farm in Iowa. They were a slow team but they wouldn't balk at a load, they'd keep pulling. It didn't take long to catch on. You turn the plow handles the opposite way you want the plow to cut and in new ground it was tough. The plow would glance off a root once in a while and you'd hit a rock, stop cold, or the shear (point of plow) would pop out. Sometimes, and why I don't know, an area would be still froze just four inches below the surface. Then after you plowed up a field, you'd take the team with a wagon and pull out roots and throw them on the wagon. By today's standards it was slow and hard work. But again when you're finished, it's satisfying to see your fields ready to plant.

   The upper half of the field I cleared the year before was about 400 x 50 feet, which is about an acre. I read in *"Draft Horse Primer"* to plow the ground, then disk it, plow it again, disk it again, and then all the ground will be chopped up the whole depth of the plow cut. But this new ground was pretty soddy. I had to do it a third time. This would be my first potato field and after dressing it up with the spike tooth harrow it was level, loose, ground. I planted half an acre in oats. Found out Athabascan or Nip Oat grew tall and made good oat hay. The other new fields I'd plant two in Timothy and one that seemed dryer in Broam, but used oats as a cover crop. I believe I planted the spuds toward the end of May and the other field maybe in the middle of May.

    I used the lister to make the rows, furrow, and spaced them about three feet apart. Then I'd drop a cut piece of spud with at least two eyes on it, spacing them fourteen or so inches apart. But as I remember, I'd run a bead of 8/32/16 fertilizer down first and lay a light dusting of dirt on it. The spuds on the dirt on fertilizer protected the seed from getting what they called "burning." Anyway, then I'd cover the row with a couple inches of dirt. I say I did this or I did that fact is, planting or harvesting, I'd get one or two guys from the church who could use a winter's worth of spuds and then we'd plant and in fall harvest and of course my kids and Adeline would pitch in. Later during the summer we'd have to cultivate and hill the rows. I always liked that work. My son would ride the horse to keep him between the rows and I'd handle the cultivator or lister to hill. It worked well and it was always good having my son working with me.

    Now that we were in the tater business we were going to need a cellar. I had an old log tent frame we weren't using. It was 10 x 12 feet. I also had a bunch of 4 x 4 timbers I didn't sell. I knew a fella from the white community of Eagle that had a backhoe. He dug a hole big enough for that 10 x 12 foot log frame to go into as well as angled up all the way to where the first door would be. At the bottom would be the second door into the actual cellar. We put plastic all around it, roofed it plastic on top, made a hole, ran a stove pipe for a vent and back-filled it, and put a couple feet of dirt on top. Later we dug a hole beside it and made a room to the original and put sixty-head of laying hens in there. I could keep the cellar averaging about forty degrees throughout the winter. Before we got electricity when it seemed to be getting a little cold in there, I'd put a kerosene lamp next to the door. Afterwards, just a 150 watt bulb would do it. The chickens needed 10 to 12 hours of light, so I'd turn the light on in the morning and off in the evening. They laid and we sold eggs and potatoes throughout the winter.

Anyway back to 1982. As it turned into July the oat hay was tall, in the milk stage, and ready to cut. I must confess, figuring out the mower and getting everything moving right was hard and some of my ground was soft and wet and it rained a lot. I got frustrated more than once trying to cut hay. Even with hay cocks it didn't turn out good and some I tried drying in the windrow but brought it in too soon. It heated up so that I had to tear into the stack and spread it around the barnyard. I knew I was going to have to buy hay that fall. It was disappointing but I learned as well. I could see I was going to need twice as much ground into hay. By the way, I seeded the field with a hand crank broadcaster. I also spread fertilizer with it. In Alaska the ground is froze most of the time and it's pretty near sterile. I tried various things in hopes of getting away from chemicals like fava bean, hairy vetch, and peas. I inoculated it but truthfully didn't get the yield we needed without fertilizer: 100 lbs. nitrogen, 50 lbs. phosphorous, and 50 lbs. potash proved good. Later as I cleared more ground I learned Garrison Creeping Foxtail was the fastest growing, highest yield, and needed less fertilizer. It looks a lot like Timothy, but has more leaf. The biggest trouble is the seed is like small feathers and floats, so spread isn't very wide, as you have to be careful.

I mentioned earlier that I had a fella from South Dakota that wanted to hunt in Alaska. That was going to happen August 20th so I decided to harvest the spuds just before the hunt. I got some help from a neighbor and of course my kids. We'd take the wagon, four buckets, and the Mitchell Potato Shaker. I'd hook the team to the shaker and they would pull it down a row, the spade would dig, the five-spoked wheel would roll along the ground making it hit the tines, making them bounce. The idea was the dirt would fall down and the spuds would roll off the top, but it seemed to me some would still get covered again. So the four of us would on hands and knees go through the dirt and pile spuds. Me or somebody else would take two buckets and pick um up, then dump um in the wagon. That would be repeated till all the rows were harvested. That first year I thought they had to air dry for a day or so. I put them in our new 14 x 14 foot addition to the barn which I'd use for the team when it gets cold. Anyway I put them in there. I forgot now how many days it took us, but I remember later years it took two or three days to do a half to three quarter acre, and seemed like we usually harvested about four tons of spuds. Then we had to move them again into the cellar. In later years we put um right in the cellar and they kept just fine through the winter. Usually in later years we harvested the spuds after Labor Day. I might say one year on new, just cleared ground I planted the spuds and only got my seed back. That Alaska ground is too cold, therefore short on bacteria to pass nutrients to plant. We plowed up sticks that had been there probably ten years or so (I'd guess) that were just in the process of rotting. But as you peel the moss off and work the ground a couple years, the frost line close to the surface disappears and it grows good hay with some fertilizer. Frost free days for growing were around the first of June to about the first week in August.

Well that hunter from South Dakota was coming and I was to meet him with the horses at a bush airstrip, which was on Alder Creek, eighty miles west of Eagle. God was going to get my attention about obeying him. In 1 Peter 2:14-15 God says, *"Obey the governing authorities."* What I was doing was breaking the law and God was going to punish me for it. You see on the trapline as a heathen I could care less about the law. I took what we needed, when we needed. God was beginning to change me to trust what He says and do what He says. But old habits sometimes are slow to stop. There was a young man who was going to buy Pappy after I got back from this hunt and was going with me to Alder Creek airstrip to get a little experience with horses. We traveled west of Eagle on the Seventymile trail which was an old winter "CAT road" to support the Seventymile gold miners. There was still some mining on the different creeks coming into the Seventymile River. They freighted out the trail usually in March while frozen, but four or five years earlier an outfit that was going to mine on Crooked Creek started in May and really tore up the trail. It would prove to be the demise of one of my horses. It was a little soft and muddy being August and when we crossed the creeks we'd come to, I noticed the youngest of the team, Dollar, was freaking out. He'd bock and then leap out into the middle of the creek. But Brian, who was riding him, only got big-eyed and held on.

As we got to what was called the Summit cabin we knew we were about ten miles from Eagle. We stopped for about a half an hour then traveled on. We were both riding and packing the older one of the team. I had two sacks of cracked barley from Delta, Alaska, our bed rolls, some grub, cooking gear, black plastic for making a hooch in case of rain, a trail axe and file, a rifle, and also a sawed off .22 for grouse or ptarmigan. It was maybe a 175 lb. pack. I used a "basket hitch" for the side bags then put on a top-load with tarp over the whole thing and laced it down with a "double diamond hitch." He proved to be a good steady packhorse.

About two hours later we came to a depression, almost a valley, and as I came to the middle I heard a running of water. Now as I said earlier a CAT train had torn up the trail badly, scraping most of the moss off and blading it to frost. The moss was coming back; that's one thing that cold, acidic ground can grow – moss. I heard that water running and saw what looked like about a foot and a half to two-foot wide mat of moss kind of hanging above the running water. Pappy just hopped across and so did Old Bob, but Dollar bocked sideways to the sound and all of a sudden dropped down in that running water. It was a crack in the permafrost and a little creek was forming about six or seven feet down, just wide enough for Dollar to drop into. Brian jumped off, but there Dollar stood about a foot below ground cover. We tried every way we could to get him out: chopping into that frozen ground with the axe, tried pulling him out with the horses, and so on. But he wouldn't even try to help himself. He was up against frozen ground and we finally figured out one back leg was busted. So I shot him in the head. That was the end of a promising team and it was also the judgement of God, the price I'd pay for breaking the law. We took the saddle off and cached it in a tree. Now one of us would be walking and one riding. It was at least an hour after dark when we made camp on some high ground. We didn't sleep to good as I remember.

Now back in Iowa, I'd taken out an insurance policy on the team for $3,000 apiece cuz I figured all the traveling and I would have that much in them and the insurance wasn't too much. But the insurance company wanted photos of Dollar. The how to do that was going to be tough. Then I remembered there was a helicopter working out of Eagle, always taking geologists out, passing over the Seventymile trail. I told Brian to ask

Adeline my wife to talk to the pilot and see if he could take Brian and my wife out there to take pictures. As it turned out, the pilot swapped a pair of Indian moccasins that my wife made and took them out to take the pictures. It was only a five minute ride out there anyway (twelve or thirteen miles). Later I would end up going all the way to Dawson Creek, B.C. and use up more than $3,000 to get another horse. More on that later, back to the story of the hunt.

It had been raining a fair bit that summer; the Seventymile River was a bit high. I'd help Brian to get up on top of the pack. I'd ride Pappy and lead Bay across. We'd point the horses a little upriver and cross on the wide stretch that was shallower. Pappy was belly deep but had footing and didn't have to swim. I can't remember how many camps it took to get to Alder Creek, maybe two or three, but I remember we went through a lot of soft ground. Pappy had the hardest time even though on soft ground we'd be afoot and ol Bay would still have the pack. Pappy wore #2 horseshoes. Bay wore #4s on the front and #3s on the back and was long in the leg where Pappy wasn't. I remember an old-timer said mules weren't as good as horses in Alaska cuz the small, narrow hoof would tend to suck in bad. I wouldn't know, as I never worked mules. Anyway we got to one place in the trail and it came to a boggy lake and the ground was soft. So we'd had it with the Seventymile trail and cut straight to the north side of the valley to the base of the hills and found it dry, but we had to bushwhack. There were caribou trails generally going the same westerly direction.

Later the valley narrowed up a bit and the CAT trail ran on higher, dryer ground so we followed it into Alder Creek and the gold mine camp. It was as I remember near dark, maybe 8:00 p.m. Sonny Mitnen and Woody Woodal were there cooking supper and we were ready to eat. They were mining with CATS, placer mining, as I remember. They were both hard drinkers and Sonny could put the fear of Sonny in a man when drunk. He was 6'5" or so and about 260 pounds but when sober, friendly enough. They didn't drink at the mine, only in town, so we slept okay and I rested up waiting for the hunter to come. There was grass, so the horses did good and rested up for a couple of days. Brian would fly back on the plane the hunter would come in on.

The hunter finally came in and being the afternoon, we spent the rest of the day organizing our outfit and discussing our hunt. I decided I didn't want to hunt the headwaters of the Seventymile cuz I'd have to go back to Eagle the same way and that was a tough road. Instead we'd head for Glacier Mountain and my old trappin country traveling east to American Summit and the gravel road to Eagle. It would be about 100 miles of rough, mountain and valley traveling but no swamps or bogs to go through. But we'd be afoot since both horses would be packing a load. The grass in September isn't strong horse feed. They do better on willow leaves that they eat but I give each horse six pounds of Delta Jct. Cracked Barley a day. So one horse was packing horse feed; the other our camp and grub. The first day and a half was mainly uphill with a lot of miles of tussocks. That's the name for frozen ground that has "heaved" up humps usually the size of volleyballs laid out next to each other for many a square mile. These humps are springy moss with a short, bushy grass growing out of them. It's worse than walking across a plowed field and it was most of the day and up the ridge between Alder Creek and Granite Creek. About ten miles up, we worked our way down to cross Granite Creek only to find the crossing pretty dangerous for horses. The creek was running through boulders two or three feet in diameter, some bigger. To find a safe crossing I walked a quarter-mile downstream. I found a crossing, maybe. We'd have to be slow and careful winding over and through those underwater boulders. I'd be praying cuz it would be easy for a horse to break a leg. Well those two horses proved to be steady. They took their time and made it across balancing on more than a few boulders. We traveled up a fork of granite toward the divide between the Seventymile drainage and Fortymile River drainage. We found a patch of small spruce with a couple dead for firewood so we made camp still on the Seventymile side, as far as I can remember.

 The next day we crossed over and skirted around North Peak and crossed the headwaters of Eureka Creek. Actually a side creek of Eureka as we were still above the timberline when we saw a lone caribou, a small bull. Meat would be good; we could start eatin fit food instead of macaroni and cheese laced with Spam.

As I remember, the wind was right and we got in easy range. The man from South Dakota drew a bead on the bull, he connected, the rest is history, and we had to unload the one pack horse that had our camp on and load him back up with meat as well as the camp.

As I recall we had to go one mile before we came across two grizzlies traveling west, as we were traveling east toward the main Eureka Creek and Glacier Mountain. Well we were on a side hill and they were on a bench, just a little lower and about 200 yards away. The South Dakotan bellied down, he had some kind of tripod on the forearm of his rifle, and he took the one with the darker pelt as I remember. That bear didn't know what hit him and dropped with one shot. The hunter wanted a full mount and did the skinnin himself. It was going to be close to dark if we wanted to make it near Glacier Peaks and sheep country. I doubt if we made it. Probably we had to make camp on Eureka. We were now in my old stompin grounds.

This country was lucky to see a man other than me in ten to twenty years. It's typical Alaskan high country, pretty but tough to walk through. Our South Dakota boy was doing okay. Though, as I remember we had to throw a little griz blood on ol Pappy's nose and put my jacket over his eyes to load that bear's hide and a little fat meat. (That country isn't salmon country and bear fatten on blueberries and such fat griz meat ain't bad.) I can picture where we would have come down to Eureka Creek, away up near the head, probably 3,200 feet. There's timber and of course willow along the creek.

There's a flat out there on the west side that has creek ice that glaciers up during the winter and gets so thick it doesn't melt all off till the end of July or so. I've seen caribou passing through there as I've camped nearby in July. They'd lie on that cool blue ice. It's a wild and pretty place but lonely too! Although that never bothered me much, I was always at home in those far off mountains with a couple good pack horses. That makes life mighty fine. I reckon I should pause and thank God He didn't give me a boring life. One can see clearly that God is the greatest artist there ever will be.

We got up in the morn and packed up. We'd only be going about four miles and camp for a few days under Glacier Peaks, west slope. We had a small tent and stove and we used it now as we'd be here three or four days. Dakota in the afternoon wanted to rest up, so I walked up to the foot of Glacier to have a look-see and sure enough a couple of young rams crossed above me over the ridge as I was walkin up. They were headed north.

Glacier Peaks, as I called it, has four different good size drainages that water pours out of. The mountain from Eureka on the west and southwest, Comet Creek on the southeast, and east these two eventually run into the Fortymile River. Then Mission Creek, north and northeast, runs directly into the Yukon River and then Mogul Creek, on the northwest side, it runs into the Seventymile. These mountains get over 6,000 feet, you'd think they're small, but they are not. The timberline is around 3,500 feet and so stick up a fair bit and they're rugged.

The next morning we put the packsaddles on the horses and Dakota rode one and I rode the other. We went northeasterly up that part of Glacier where I saw the sheep headed the day before. We were going up a long, low ridge that eventually, just before the crest of the northwest side of Glacier Mountain, got steep. We tied the two horses to each other's packsaddle up short. There's no brush to tie to up there and the worst they can do is turn in a circle but they generally just stand. We walked up to the crest and looked into Excelsior Creek which is part of Mission Creek. There were thirteen rams down there. Seven were 7/8ths to full curl which are legal rams. While we were glassing these we happened to look back at the horses and saw on a bench on the west side of the ridge we came up there were two legal rams. Laying down these would be easy to get, the others pretty tough being down in another drainage. So we turned back toward the horses that were below the top of the ridge opposite the rams, then snuck over and got on the top and bellied down to within maybe 75 yards or so. Dakota laid there, flipped out his tripod on his rifle and put the crosshairs on the bigger of the two and took his shot. It was a 7/8 curl, not real big, but not bad either. He was happy.

It was of Fannin tendencies. What I mean is a Stone ram bread a Dall ewe somewhere back in its family tree cuz there was a fair bit of gray hair on its sides. The Stone sheep are mainly hanging out in northern B.C., Canada but a few slip on into the central Yukon Territory which is close. I imagine this sheep's grand pap wandered into these mountains and fell in love with a Dall ewe and the rest is history.

We shoved the ram over the side and let it roll down to the valley. There weren't much rock and mainly a mossy steep hill to the valley below that would take us to camp. Dakota wanted a full mount so he got busy skinnin. I went after the horses and brought them to the sheep. We packed the sheep and hide and headed back to camp. We now had caribou meat, a little bear meat, and a sheep. That was just a start in my family's winter meat and we probably would have that polished off by October. We'd need more but there's a good feeling when you make meat. I guess that's why I never felt guilty when I was still a heathen before I was saved. We didn't hunt for sport. Something had to die for my family and dog team to eat. So to follow the law didn't come easy. But I'd pay in for my sin having to beat the snow coming and going to Dawson Creek, B.C. to get a replacement for the horse I lost before I got back. I used up all the insurance money as well as some of my own.

Anyway, we got to camp and I cooked up some sheep tongue and rice as well as fried up some kidneys. After we ate up some of the guts, we'd eat fry meat and rice in the morning and fry meat, gravy, and some bannock bread at supper. Usually we didn't eat in the middle of the day on the trail. I never got tired of the feed and I work well on it too. We slept well that night to wake up to snow and wind. I'd originally planned to skirt around the south side of Glacier Mountain but the weather stopped us. In a whiteout in the mountains you can get turned around easy so now the best thing to do is travel down Eureka Creek the twenty-odd miles to my Main cabin on the trapline. I've been on this trail many a time. It would be good to see the old place.

All bush trails in Alaska are on the tough side compared to the lower 48, but this trail isn't bad just another long day of walking. Thanks to the horses we don't have to pack this load on our backs. I've memories of packing 100 pound packs on this trail. We came into the yard of the Main cabin just before dark. We had to set up the stove and stovepipe and get a fire going. There was plenty grass around the cabin for the horses. Ol Bay was a wanderer so I always staked him out on a rope and hobbled Pappy with a horse bell on his neck. What with cracked barley they did good on the trail. There's something special about coming to one of these cabins at the end of a long, tough day and getting a fire going. It must be like a sailor making a safe harbor after coming through a storm. The weather had gotten a little better and the snow in the upper reaches of Eureka was rain in the lower reaches but as I recall it stopped later in the day. Walking with rain gear keeps ya dry but ya get hot. We were there at my first home that had a lot of memories of my wife and kids out there with me. It was good to be back if only for a night.

The next morning we ate, packed horses, and went the mile or so to the mouth of Eureka Creek and followed the North Fork of the Fortymile River for about two miles and turned up Comet Creek. I had a pretty good trail up this creek cuz this was the way into my country from Eagle in the winter and summer about ten to eleven miles up. I've a cabin across from a moose lick. A moose lick is a mineral spring with the dirt having salt in it. They paw at the dirt and lick it. There's a lot of grass there. We let the horses eat and we looked at the lick and the old line cabin. Little did I know, but in the following couple of years, my son and I and four horses would come out here and kill a moose: a bull with 3" of fat on his butt and a 60" rack. I'll write about that later.

We made it to the upper cabin on Comet Creek. It's just below the timberline next to the east slopes of Glacier Mountain. From where we shot the sheep to there was probably fifteen or so miles but that fifteen miles has about three major ups and downs and a lot of side hills and brush. The weather was bad so it felt like we traveled maybe 40 miles. This cabin site has been used since about 1900. There were several remains of old caches. They're handy to keep bears and squirrels out. Caches are little cabins built on a couple good size trees topped off at sixteen feet or so and they keep your outfit dry. From time to time a lot of caribou pass through here. I've seen over 1,000 in one bunch and others scattered all over.

The next morning we headed east on my summer trail that ends up on American Summit where a gravel road called the Taylor Highway crosses to Eagle. It's good mountain horse country running mainly ridges and going above the timberline then back down then back up and so on. It's about twenty-five miles. I think we made camp a few miles from the road cuz we'd be walking down the road to Eagle, another seventeen miles. I think we made a roundtrip of over 200 miles from Eagle and back. Dakota was pleased but I felt guilty and judged by God by losing that horse and I know I have a long, hard trip ahead to replace him. That was sure a good team. It was going to be hard but I'd be trying to obey the game laws from now on.

I got home somewhere around the middle of September. There was some oat hay on cocks to bring in and many other chores before winter and maybe some custom sawmill cutting for somebody I recall. But the dreaded trip to Dawson Creek, B.C., to get a replacement horse was on the horizon. I tried to use Pappy with Bay. It wasn't working but I did get the hay in.

I hate to go into the whole trip down and back, I pretty much explained the trip up from Iowa. So I'll just talk about the horse I'd heard about when I was working for guides from a man who boarded their horses and also sold horses. Can't remember his name now, but I'd called him and he said he had a 1,400 lb. black part-Percheron mare he'd sell. He said he had done some skidding with her. Well if I was going to have a team to use in the woods, I better do it soon or the Taylor Highway was going to be closed for the winter. We came back to Eagle in a snowstorm. I seem to recall a few drifts we punched through. I also bought hay and oats to bring back because I sure didn't have enough hay.

The mare wasn't supposed to be bred but come spring plowing, I could see she was. She was bulky pulling, she wouldn't back, and I'd have to break her to do both. I told earlier how I taught Pappy to pull. I did the same with her. The backing I'd never had to break a horse, the team from Iowa did so. I studied on it. First just harness with lines, she wouldn't budge. So I got my son to pull on the lines and I literally put my shoulder in her chest and pushed her back. I'm sure there's a better way but she started to back some, then caught on, and backed up. Next I put her in a single horse wagon I'd built for hauling water and so on. She wouldn't want to and I worked on her about most of a day before she would back but she learned and so did I. She was at least 250 lbs. lighter and a good four or five inch shorter and quicker on the start than ol Bay. More than a few times they seesawed the evener back and forth before they'd get a heavy load started. But by the middle of winter they were good enough and we got the winter work done.

But I'm jumpin ahead a little. It's still October and we don't have the mill out in the woods yet. This year I wouldn't need a CAT to haul out the boards. I was finally independent for transport. It'd be all horsepower for moving logs and lumber. We were going to be in the same area this year about four miles from our home place. Steve Hamilton was going to work with me again but, as I remember, he couldn't go with me to start. So I had to hire one of the boys from the village for a week or so. We had to extend the road out about a half a mile farther and clear an area for the sawmill and log deck. The bobsled was no longer set up with shafts, but had a tongue put on using two inch pipe for a team of horses to pull. I could now haul a cord of wood or put a box on it and haul freight or lumber or in this case, a sawmill. I could load the mill, tent, stove, and other necessaries for work in one shot. Things were going right. *"Praise the Lord."*

The routine was in morning, after reading the Word and praying, I'd go feed and harness the horses. Then Adeline would have breakfast ready for the kids and me. The kids would walk a half-mile to catch the bus for school and Steve would show up about 8:30 a.m. and shortly thereafter hitch the team to the bobsled and about an hour later be out to the sawmill. We'd unhook the sled at the head of the sawmill to easily stack lumber in the sled, tie the horses to a tree, and get the stove pipe wired under the oil pan of the mill. I'd light up a propane torch and set it in the stove pipe. That would safely heat up the mill engine in about 15 or 20 minutes. We'd also start the wood stove in the wall tent in case we needed a warm place to sharpen the chainsaw, eat lunch, and also warm up the chainsaw a little as well as the chain oil. The mill's gas tanks would run about 2 ½ hours. We'd saw one tank in the morning and cut about 600 board feet of lumber, eat lunch, and sharpen the saw. Steve would go out and start dropping trees, limbing, and bucking logs.

Any trail work I'd get one of the horses rigged up with a singletree log chain and lines for one horse skidding and head out to skid what Steve had ready. I had a scaling stick and scale logs as we bought that to deck in front of the mill and skid till we had about 600 or so board feet of logs. Usually twelve logs since the timber in the Alaska interior aren't real big. The butt cut first log at 16' averaged 11" at the small end, some larger, some smaller of course. By 3:00 or 3:30 p.m. we would head for the barn. Steve would go home but those kids of mine would be home from school and would help me unload lumber in the lumber yard, unharness the horses, put um in the stable, and give um a can of Delta Junction cracked barley and a manger full of hay. Later I'd come out and water them after supper.

We'd do it five days a week. Saturday I'd do chores, haul water, and repair anything that needed to be done. The kids would help so that way Adeline wouldn't be bothered while she baked bread for the week. Saturday was pinto beans and fresh rolls and Saturday night baths in our wash tub. Sunday we'd hitch the team to the wagon for church which was four miles down the road. We'd visit some after church and take our time going home.

We'd usually start sawing in mid-October till the first week or so in December then shut down the mill till around the first of February then saw till the first week or so of April. December and January are too dark and too cold to saw. I'd stay close to home.

However, the last three years of the 80s decade I had a different routine that was quite diversified. The farm was paying for itself which was feed for the horses and goats, and spuds for us. Selling potatoes paid for seed and fertilizer. I found it was cheap to mail 50 lb. bags of seed (oats) and fertilizer rather than going to Delta Junction and trucking it in on the thirteen acres of hay. I'd use 100 lbs. nitrogen, 50 lb. of phosphorous, and 50 lbs. of potash. We'd get about a ton and a half of yield per acre whether Oat Hay or Garrison Creeping Foxtail. (The latter was hard to seed but the perennials the earliest to cut, best yield, and hardest to die out.) For potatoes I use 8 lbs. nitrogen, 32 lbs phosphorous and 16 lbs. potash and we'd get a good yield of spuds. We'd fertilize and plant in May. This is what we called field work: plowing, disking, and harrowing.

Also we'd been burning the "berm piles." That's the moss, trees, and brush that got piled up by the CAT as we were first clearing the fields. It was shaping up to be a pretty fair operation *"Praise the Lord."* It wasn't without blood, sweat, and tears literally but at last I was beginning to know what I was doing. The living we were making had a horse's foot involved in every dollar we made. I liked that satisfying work and we were "tough to starve out." We'd burn in October. The berm piles would smolder all winter. By the first of May with team, a slip, and a harrow we'd clear off most of the berm piles by 1986. It took about four years to develop our fields of about 14 acres. Twelve acres were in grass hay, an acre in oat hay and an acre in potatoes. That mare that I bought in Dawson Creek, B.C., was pregnant and threw a filly. The next year I sold her, knowing I could sell hay to her new owners each fall cuz I was harvesting enough hay for my three horses, milk goat, plus enough for a fourth horse so again I was making some cash money.

As I said earlier, May was field work, June I'd be selling lumber, building anything that needed building, also weeding potatoes, and toward the end of June cultivating spuds. July was haying month as well as the King Salmon were running up the river. I'd run the nets with my son or daughter. I had a 16-foot aluminum riverboat with a 15 hp. Johnson on it. We'd do this in the morning cuz I'd be haying the rest of the day if it wasn't raining. Because of the rain it usually took most of the month to put up hay or at least get it on haycocks; some I'd finish stacking in September.

We now had enough land fenced off for the horses to graze every night in June and July. I'd bring um in for the day and put um in the corral in case I needed them. In August they either would be with me in the mountains huntin or I'd put them on my hay land once I'd cut. They'd eat the stubble up by the first week of October then dine on feed hay till next June. August was huntin. I'd learned my lesson to be honest and follow the game laws. I found that I could find somebody in one of the cities of Alaska that wanted to hunt sheep. I could do that honestly since they were residents. So August 10th through the 20th I'd take a hunter or two with my horses out to Glacier Mountains. I did that from 1985 to 1988. It paid good and I'd usually get the meat and we'd also kill a caribou or two.

Fall in those mountains starts in mid-August. It doesn't take long till the country is full of reds and yellows and it sure is beautiful.

In some of those later years of the 80s during the first part of September there were caribou coming within five or six miles of the road to Eagle. It was timberline country and I'd take my son and a friend of his and we'd each shoot a bull caribou for winter meat. We had electricity so we had a freezer. With the king salmon, caribou, and sheep we would do okay. A few of those years we'd get a moose too. Fall was harvest time for hunting, farm potatoes, and Adeline's big garden. She'd put away carrots, blanched cauliflower, broccoli, and cabbage. The carrots went into in five-gallon buckets of moist sand then she put um in the cellar along with spuds, kippered salmon, blueberry jam, and cranberries. Cauliflower and broccoli we'd put in the freezer. So we ate pretty good along with the eggs and goat milk. Also in September I'd hire Jack Boone because he had a truck with a box on it. He'd go to Delta Junction and bring back four tons of coarse ground barley. That was enough for a year for the horses, goat, and sixty chickens we had. (I'd feed ½ layers mash and ½ barley.)

As soon as it snowed in October, I'd take the team three abreast, the bobsled, chainsaw, saw gas and oil, and start cutting and hauling cordwood for my family. I needed one load per month, one cord of heater wood: Birch, Black Spruce, and Aspen (green). We'd use the slabs for our cook stove. I'd also sell 25 cords a winter at $100 a cord. I'd cut and haul out a "honest cord" a day. I would do that three or four days a week. Every Thursday I'd take a wagon to town and deliver eggs and potatoes. By this time the local garbage dump was near our farm. I'd pick up garbage from some of the people in town and haul it back out so even the back haul was paid. The Lord provided. He said to Adam, *"You shall work by the sweat of your brow."* I found that to be true but it's been satisfying to sort out and carve out a life off the land and provide something useful for your community.

By 1985 I finally had the right horses. What happened horse-wise I'll explain as follows:

In 1980 got the single horse Pappy, then in January 1982 in Iowa I got the team, lost Dollar on the trail to Seventymile in August, and bought the black part-Percheron mare in October 1982.

In 1983 I bought the colt I saw over by White Horse, Yukon Territory, Canada. In the meantime the mare threw a filly that I sold. That stud colt in 1983 was two-years-old and I bred him to the mare. Her name was Blaze. That same year in June, Bay had been staked out on some grass. I think he got tangled up and tore his stifle tendon. He could do light work but not heavy. I took him to Fairbanks and sold him. He did buggy rides there. I bought a small team in Wassila, Alaska and used them that winter logging and the following spring doing field work then took them in the fall to Delta and sold them.

In 1984 the colt from Canada was three-years-old. I

broke him and used him that summer. Also with that little team I borrowed Pappy back and I went out that fall to the moose lick on Comet Creek with my son and shot a bull moose, 60" fat. The mare Blaze threw a nice stud colt; a bay like his father. I had these three: Blaze, Jack (the colt from Canada), and Jake. I had Jack and Jake cut so both were geldings. They grew into about 1,700 lb. horses. The three horses did a lot of work for me there in Eagle and then logging in Wyoming for five years, and then back to Copper Center, Alaska for six more years. I sold them eventually and went overseas to Mongolia to serve the Lord there.

But back to our little homestead on the Yukon River. As I said earlier, December and January are short on light and long on cold, so we stayed close to the farm, did chores and burned lots of wood. It keeps ya from getting bored. Speaking of chores, the sixty-head of chickens kept my kids in chores. We added onto the potato cellar and I strung an electric line there. I had one 200-watt bulb beside the inside door to the first room where the spuds were along with a thermometer. If it dropped below 35 degrees, I'd turn that light on. The second light was in the chicken room. I'd keep that on twelve hours a day. It gave them enough light to lay eggs through the winter. In their room it stayed 45 degrees most of the time.

After school my kids would gather eggs, feed and water the chickens, shovel manure into buckets, and pack it to the manure pile by the stable. In the manure pile we also threw fish guts and heads and in the summer when the chickens were loosed they would scratch and pick at it. In the winter it was steaming all winter so it cooked (composted) good. Adeline's big garden was fed with it and I'd put the rest on the spud patch. But it just wouldn't spread far. I couldn't even cover a quarter of it and in Alaska the ground is just too cold. I had to use chemical fertilizer.

My first barn burnt down in July of 1986. A friend of mine asked to put a freezer there and fill it with king salmon. I noticed it was making funny noises one day as I saddled a horse to go check on something. I had gotten a little ways away when a niece of ours came running and yelling, *"The barn's on fire."* I whipped and spurred back but was only able to save a set of harnesses and the hay stacks. I'd gone out for a week with the Eagle Fire Crew to fight a forest fire ten miles downriver and thought we'd have a little extra money. I had to use that to regroup and rebuild. But *"Praise the Lord"* I had that money for this mistake and *"Praise the Lord"* I had a sawmill!

I decided not to put all my eggs in one basket so I laid out my new farm buildings as follows: my corral was in the center of the barnyard and was eight-sided and had 16 feet between the posts. It was five poles high with the top pole being head high. On the northeast side I built a 10' x 12' stable. I had a piece of plywood for a window on the north side so I could pitch out the manure. On the east side I had a window with a tarp over it to pitch hay for the three horses into the hay manger. The hay stacks were fenced in on the east side of the stable and corral so the horses or goat couldn't get to them but were close enough to feed easily.

On the southeast corner of the corral a little back, I had a combination grain shed/goat shed. There was a wall between the goat and the grain with a door made up of 1" x 6" x 18" stacked up so the grain lowered as I fed it out to the livestock. I had a door in part of the roof that I could take out and by bucket I could fill it. The grain truck would back up to it so one guy could scoop up a bucket then pass it up to the guy sitting on the roof who dumped the grain in. I had the studs on the outside, the boards on the inside, and I tacked burlap on the inside so no grain could leak out. The goat room also had a doghouse in there so the goat's body heat would keep her warm. I had a milking station with a little hay manger so that she could feed while I milked her. She pretty well dried up by November and usually threw a couple kids in March. I'd either borrow a buck or use her son. Then I killed him. One doe was enough for us as we had milk about eight months a year.

The tack shack was on the southwest corner of the corral. I had saddles, packsaddles, harnesses, shoeing tools, etc. in there. The corral gate was between the tack shack and the grain shed. This ended up a pretty practical setup. Those last four years I had the sawmill set up a little east of the barnyard. I'd already been stacking lumber there. There was a little uphill roll to the ground. I set the sawmill next to it and put the saw log uphill of it, so I could easily roll logs to the mill. There was plenty of room to come in with the team and bobsled loads of logs.

In between the mill yard and barnyard I had the cellar and Adeline's garden. To the west of the barnyard was our house. I had a fence from the riverbank to the creek bank. The fence was probably 100 yards long. The creek bank and riverbank were both steep so it kept the horses and goats out until the grass needed mowing. Then I'd let them in. It worked out well, high enough it would generally not flood although a couple times it did just a little. Adeline kept flowers in the yard on the side of the house. It was kind of pretty. On a summer eve it was nice sitting on the porch watching the river roll by.

About February, I'd start thinking about logging. Those years I'd log by myself. There wasn't any one stand of trees where I could set up the mill and log all winter; just maybe twenty saw log trees here and there. The rest was Birch, Aspen, Black or Scrub Spruce, and Brush. I'd buy 10,0000 board feet each of those last three winters and hunt out those little islands like patches of saw timber. I could generally get 500 board feet of logs on the bobsled each day. About twenty day's work would see us finished up. Logging in March was pleasant except the snow was usually thigh deep. The sun was high enough to warm most of the afternoons to about 15 degrees above zero and the days were a little longer too.

I did always cut a trail, or rather a road, to where the timber was and make a landing or deck big enough to skid logs beside the bobsled. I cut pole thick enough to set on the bob's bunks to roll logs onto the bob with the cant hook. When the first layer filled the bunk I'd then put the rollers on top the outside log and roll the next row up on them and so on. So I'd end up with kind of a pyramid shape. Around the center of the load I'd use the log chain and tighten it with a come-along. The road was usually rough so the logs had to be tight. I usually used the team to skid these logs in March. The snow was deep but once the skid trail was busted out it would freeze overnight. From then on the horses didn't flounder so much.

I did tie up the team when I'd first get to the timber. Then take a chainsaw and knock down four or five trees that would make about 500 board feet of logs. That part of Alaska, usually the trees had a 16' butt cut, then a 12' and an 8.' I'd keep it 21' marked to buck in to two logs at the deck to load up on the bobsled, so usually three saw logs per tree 16 foot, 12 foot, and 8 foot or one 16 foot and two 10 foot and sometimes two 16 foot or three 12 foot. It varied depending on the taper of the tree. It was never a long day. If I left the barn at 9:30 a.m., I'd be back by 3:30 or 4:00 p.m. in the afternoon. But that's okay. By the time I unloaded logs, tended to the horses, and did other chores the day was used up.

Usually at the end of March I'd have the logging done and then in April the snow would start to melt and it would get muddier as April turned toward May. That month I'd stay at home running the sawmill. On Thursday I'd take eggs and spuds to town. By the first of May I'd finish milling out lumber. By then the local people would be thinking about building projects and

I'd be ready for them.

That was a year's cycle for the horses and us. Hooves were involved in about all of it. I even used them to move lumber into various piles depending on lengths and width and spread sawdust with the slip. Those were good years and a good place to raise our kids. They weren't without pain and challenges but there's no place to get away from that on this sin-cursed earth. I've learned to be thankful for those special moments and be trusting God through the trials.

Contentment with what we have is a blessing. But also a vision for what can be with the right kind of effort is important. Life for man without a vision for the future must be a sad thing. I don't know cuz God has always given me a vision for something to work for or toward and He's made me a little more useful for His kingdom as life goes on. I see now that life is to give and not to take.

It took all parts of the year's cycle to make a living for the family. If any one part was missing we'd be short but God provided and for about those last four years things went well. But along about February of 1989 God was giving me another vision, both to be curious what the Christian life was like outside of Eagle, Alaska and what the western United States was like. It would be good to be around other horsemen and I'd like to get to a country where I could do some real horse logging. So with quite a few phone calls and studying the maps and a fair bit of praying, we loaded up what outfit we'd need. We made sure the old stock truck was running right, loaded the three horses, and with the two kids and wife we turned another chapter in our life. We'd spend the next five years in Wyoming.